D1381269

WILDLIFE
GARDENING

First published in Great Britain in 2003 by Cassell Illustrated,
a Division of Octopus Publishing Group Limited,
2-4 Heron Quays, London E14 4JP

Distributed in the United States of America by
Sterling Publishing Co., Inc.,
387 Park Avenue South, New York, NY 10016-8810

A CIP catalogue record for this book is available from the British
Library.

ISBN 1 84403 035 0

Printed in China

The Daily Telegraph

WILDLIFE
GARDENING

CHARLIE RYRIE

CASSELL
ILLUSTRATED

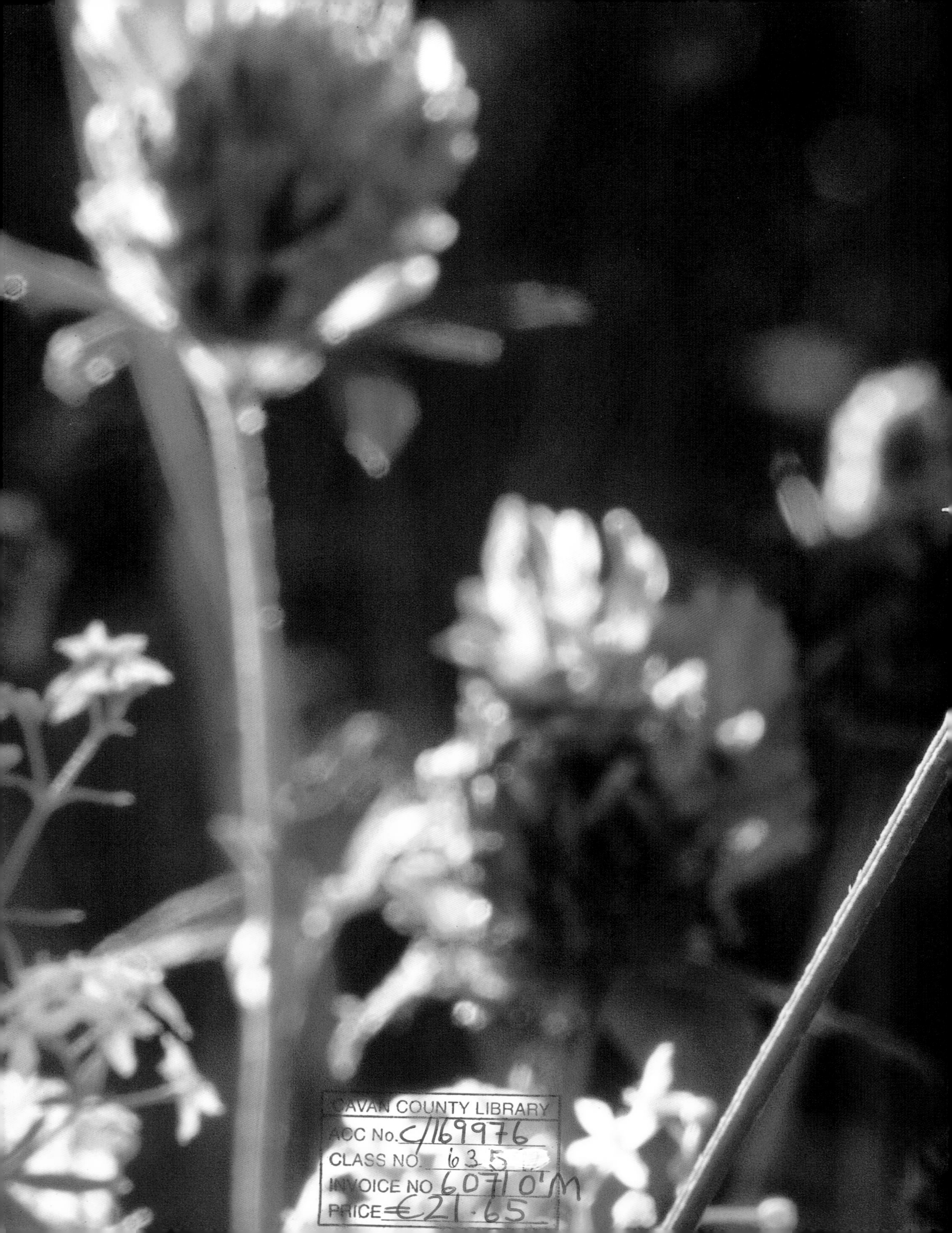

Contents

Introduction

We are a nation of gardeners. Gardening seems to be part of our national psyche, and whenever we have time to spare we flock to visit gardens and open spaces, we frequent garden centres and nurseries at weekends, and we rush to buy the numerous gardening magazines which fill newsagents' shelves. You can scarcely turn on the television without stumbling on a gardening programme.

This should not be a surprise, as gardening is accessible to almost everyone. But rather than just considering the superficial look of our gardens, with a bit of imagination and basic understanding we can make them even more special and enjoyable, by ensuring they are accessible to wildlife. There is huge pleasure to be gained from a garden alive with the sound of birdsong, the croaking of toads and frogs, as well as the spectacle of butterflies and busy insects. This enjoyment comes from more than the delight in getting "back to nature", it is the knowledge that you really are helping to conserve our native wildlife which is so satisfying.

These wild creatures need our help. We have systematically destroyed so many habitats over the past fifty years, that many creatures and plants have not been able to survive and the existence of others is now threatened. The demise of some species, including butterflies and bats, has been carefully charted, and we know of the disappearance of certain wildflowers; however, there is no way of knowing how many lesser-noticed species we have lost.

Every single living thing is part of a chain, a web of life; each link supports another link. We do not understand all these connections, and have not even named millions of species in this chain; however, it is entirely possible that some tiny organisms, such as algae or single-celled bacteria, may play a crucial role that we have no way of estimating. In other words the loss of any species may have vital significance to the balance of life.

It is easy to bemoan the extinction of a beautiful butterfly that we enjoyed watching in childhood, and it is an obvious indicator of the need for action, but unsung species are just as vital. And just as our gardens are important for wildlife, so wildlife is important for our gardens. Microscopic creatures keep the soil in good condition so that it will support healthy plants, that will support insects, that will feed birds, that will control pests and pollinate our trees, which provide fruit – everything is linked, and the more links we preserve the healthier our gardens will be.

Thirty years ago the idea of gardening for wildlife would have been laughed at. Gardens provided flowers, fruit and vegetables, and anything that might conceivably stand in the way of production was relentlessly despatched. This was the era of chemical warfare, the "if it moves, kill it" mentality. It was a mentality promoted by the ever-increasing availability of pesticides, herbicides and fungicides, the vast array encouraging gardeners to reach for the spray at the first sign of damage.

As agriculture became ever more dependent on chemicals to realise its dreams of mass production, horticulture followed in its wake. Organic farming was only for those who could not afford chemicals, anyone interested in sustainable land management was considered a definite weirdo; organic gardening did not exist officially – although of course cottage and country gardeners had always practised it.

Increased road building and urbanisation have been two factors destroying huge chunks of habitat, but our attitude to the land is massively to blame. The drive for mechanisation and expansion in agriculture after the Second World War arose out of a genuine desire and need to up production, but the methods were savage. Agricultural "improvements" led to widespread and large scale habitat and species losses – not just caused by the devastating effects of chemical use but also by drainage of wetlands and ponds, uprooting of hedgerows and the clearing of traditional woodland. Reforestation with densely planted conifer crops, with the subsequent loss of wildflowers, butterflies and songbirds, and the replacement of traditional meadows with modern ryegrass pasture, which contains so few species compared with the diversity of traditional grasslands, compounded the damage.

In the past century traditional meadows have decreased by over 80 per cent in northern Europe. As grazing requirements and patterns have changed other grassland has also became degraded, upland moors have been too often overgrazed, thanks to subsidised over-stocking, while lowland heaths have increasingly been undergrazed and overgrown. As a result lowland heathland is now comparatively rare – covering less than 20 per cent of the area it covered in the 1930s.

Field sizes have increased over the years. This has caused the loss of nearly 400,000 kilometres/250,000 miles of hedgerows, in Britain alone, since the 1960s, and small woodlands have all but disappeared. Even where old woodland remains, it is very rare to find it managed in the traditional way by coppicing, which is the ideal management technique to support hosts of insects, birds, butterflies and wildflowers. Moreover, invasive non-native species have taken hold in many areas, crowding out the plants that many species of insect relied on. As the insects vanish, so too do all the species that prey on them – carnivorous insects and birds in particular.

Damp meadows were also casualties of the increase in field sizes, suffering the effects of drainage and agricultural pollution. Marsh and bog-land has suffered the same fate.

Opposite page: Mixed grassland is a versatile habitat for butterflies and hosts of small creatures.

In the past fifty years more than 50 per cent of Britain's lowland fens have been lost. Peat bogs have been additionally endangered through peat mining, while new drainage and water systems have meant the loss of country ponds. Ponds are very unstable environments, prone to silting up and becoming overgrown if they are not looked after, so they have been all too easy for farmers or developers to reclaim for dry land.

The increase in field sizes and disappearance of hedges and wetlands has meant the fragmentation and loss of habitats. Take away a hedgerow and you remove a corridor for wildlife to move through, as well as a place to feed and shelter, which is especially crucial for slow-moving creatures and for linear feeders, such as bats. Remove a patch of woodland and the creatures that lived there may have a long way to travel to another. And even if the new woodland can support them, it may not have the surrounding habitats they need.

Habitats in isolation are always fragile, for when species are split into disconnected pockets their existence becomes threatened. Urbanisation and building programmes have been responsible for the most serious fragmentation of habitats, and this is where the role of urban and suburban gardeners becomes particularly important, in providing links between habitats, wildlife corridors that provide safe passage between habitats.

Thankfully, our attitudes have changed and at the beginning of the twenty-first century there is a widespread awareness of the importance of looking after our natural heritage. We miss the sight of wildflowers speckling our meadows, and hedges dripping with wild roses and autumn fruits, we would like to walk through a woodland glade and hear a nightingale sing, we want to see butterflies floating like airy angels over our flowerbeds, to welcome croaking frogs and to watch flurries of birds darting in and out of the vegetation. We even want to see insects flitting over our flowerbeds, something that would have made a previous generation reach for the spray. Much of our wildlife is in crisis since we have lost many of our traditional and ancient habitats in the countryside, and it will never be possible to recreate them all. However, there is hope.

Conservationist Miriam Rothschild was the first to show that the barren environment of a modern rye grass pasture could be transformed into a wildflower meadow. By planting and sowing appropriate wildflowers and reinstating a summer cutting and winter grazing regime, she created a meadow teeming with life.

Since this experiment in the 1970s, wildflower meadows have become desirable features – Prince Charles boasts one of the finest at Highgrove. The campaigning naturalist Chris Baines has inspired countless numbers of people ever since he first exhibited a wildflower garden at Chelsea in 1985; now you can purchase wild plants in nearly every garden centre, and almost every show garden includes a wild garden or an area of weeds and wildflowers.

The Woodland Trust and other forestry organisations all have projects to remove the smothering canopies of evergreens from old woodland and allow the native vegetation of the woodland floor to re-establish itself – which it is doing with alacrity. Organisations such as The Coppicing Project are planting thousands of acres of new woodland to be managed the traditional way. The Wildlife Trust has created showcase wildlife gardens around the country, and the Wildfowl and Wetland Trust has created a magnificent 55 hectare/136 acre wetland by the River Thames just outside London.

Enlightened schools are replacing formal spaces with ponds and meadows, and there is a vogue for creating spaces specifically with wildlife in mind. Organisations devoted to environmental regeneration, including Groundwork, are turning derelict industrial sites into new parks and open spaces where skylarks congregate, wildflowers proliferate and people play.

It has been inspiring working on this book and discovering the depth of the commitment that some people show to wildlife gardening, and the beautiful gardens they are creating. We are waking up to wildlife, and gardeners really can make a difference.

Moving forward

We cannot bring back the creatures we have lost, but we can definitely stem the flow of destruction and so prevent the loss of more. Gardens cannot provide everything that some species of wildlife need, nature is too complex to be reproduced on a miniature

Above: A small pond surrounded by abundant planting transforms any garden into a haven for wildlife.

Opposite page: Herbs lure insects, and tobacco plants are favourites for moths.

Above: Blue tits are among the commonest visitors to bird feeders.

Opposite page: A honeybee collecting pollen from a runner bean flower.

scale, but even the smallest wildlife garden can provide an island of support. Private gardens in Britain cover an astonishingly large area – well over 400,000 hectares/ 1 million acres. Then there are balconies, roofs, small courtyards and odd spaces that also provide growing opportunities. Add to that the thousands more hectares of public parks and gardens run by local authorities and national organisations, and you can see the huge potential for wildlife havens.

Gardens are unlike any natural habitat, though they share features with many. They usually display a wide range of species within a small area, and generally provide a good deal more shelter and food than would be available in the wild. Most gardeners passionately encourage floral diversity and cram their gardens with a huge variety of deliberately selected plant species, along with the weeds and wildflowers that may occur naturally. Many also welcome a variety of different spaces and divisions within one garden. These may include ponds and hedges, as well as paved areas, flower and vegetable beds, shrubs and trees.

Any garden with a good range of different plants and spaces can be perfect for wildlife, and it need not be a huge leap to change a conventionally managed garden into one that you can share happily with a variety of wild creatures. The most important first step is to lay off the chemical inputs. You certainly do not have to go wild and change an ordered space into an unkempt jungle, as virtually any type of garden can happily be adapted into a haven for wildlife; it is just a matter of understanding the principles and building on them.

If there is one change you should make, it is to try and think more like an ecologist than a gardener, and to try to understand the connections between plants and living creatures and the way your actions influence the well-being of both. Think twice before you clear away leaves or decayed plants from your borders, they could be sheltering all sorts of creatures. Think before you prune trees or hedges, if you prune at the wrong time there may be birds nesting there. If you clear a pond do not immediately remove the weed but leave it on the ground by the water for a day, so giving any aquatic creatures you have cleared out with it the chance to get back into the water.

As you get to know the creatures in your garden many more considerations may enter the picture. You may decide to create specific habitats for unsung invertebrates, or find yourself paying particular attention to the life cycle of a particular butterfly or the needs of a bat. Wildlife gardening is a gradual process, and your understanding will increase as more creatures come into your garden. The range of wildlife you can attract and host in your garden will depend on the size and situation of your plot, the habitats you can provide and whether there are complementary ones nearby. Town gardens are at least as important as those in the country, and a suburban garden with a native tree or two, plenty of ground cover, a wide variety of nectar-filled flowers and autumn berries, and a regime without pesticides and herbicides provides welcome habitats for insects and birds. You may feel that you garden in isolation, but to wildlife your garden is part of a much larger map, with one green space linked to other green spaces that may provide some or all of the features different species need.

A tiny urban garden near a public park, for example, may not be able to offer breeding opportunities to many creatures, but it may provide the food some creatures need, while the park provides the cover and shelter and places to breed. Parks may boast mature trees, hedgerows, water and shrubberies, as well as flowerbeds and large areas of grass, and although many are still managed under a traditional regime of tidiness and chemical use that reduces their hospitality, some councils have taken steps to help wildlife. This may mean they have changed mowing patterns to allow

wildflowers to spring up in selected patches – bringing advantages to butterflies, grasshoppers and hordes of insects while also reducing the maintenance and labour costs. It does not take a sea change to transform parks into attractive habitats for a much wider range of wildlife than many gardens can support.

Yet it is not just parks and gardens which are important. Every green space complements others. An unassuming patch of scruffy wasteland may not look as though it is much of a bonus to local gardens, but such sites often provide all sorts of opportunities for insects, mammals and butterflies as they are usually full of weeds, scrubby brambles and self-sown tree seedlings, all of which offer shelter and food. Enhance this habitat by filling your garden with flowers for nectar, food for birds, and, of course, water, and you may have a surprising range of wild visitors.

Every single garden, even if it is only a windowbox or hanging basket, can act as a café or watering hole for visiting creatures, and may even be able to provide a home for others. The more green and growing spaces we can create in towns, the more wildlife will move in and use these as havens and corridors for travelling from space to space. The advantages are not just to the wildlife, encouraging creatures into town gardens is a worthwhile and fascinating way of keeping in touch with nature.

One way of approaching wildlife gardening is to decide what creatures you want

Left: Bright yellow Inula is a dramatic food plant for this peacock butterfly.

Opposite page: Traditional cottage gardens attract insects, butterflies, birds and ground-dwelling creatures.

to attract and then manage your garden accordingly. Be realistic and also realise that you do not have to have open access for all – no gardener wants rabbits devastating their vegetables or rats stealing the bird food. You can keep unwanted wildlife out without resorting to poisons. For example you can fence rabbits out and keep rats away by practising good hygiene and management. The one problem with rabbit proof fencing is that if you do leave a gate open and a rabbit gets in it will not be able to get out. I was amused to visit one garden which had been designed with wildlife in mind and where this had happened. The gardener had eventually trapped the culprit after it had been destroying his plants for a week. Instead of releasing it back into the wild he despatched it and served it up for supper, declaring: "It's been eating all my plants, so now I'm eating it."

The mammals you may attract will depend largely on the size of your garden. You need a big garden to host a badgers' sett or foxes' den. Foxes and badgers have a very wide 'home range' within which they will travel and search for food, and they may be based in the countryside from where they venture into the urban environment. However, increasing numbers live in the rougher urban habitats, including railway banks, waste ground or woodland shelterbelt.

Grey squirrels also cover quite a large area in their search for food and they are increasingly common in towns, particularly in the suburbs or near parks with tall trees. Hedgehogs, shrews, voles and mice live happily in town or country gardens, they often have a home in one garden and a feeding area that extends over several. Hedgehogs can cover over three-quarters of a kilometres/half a mile in one night and a bowl of dog food will attract them into your garden, where they may well stay if you provide water, as well as a suitable place to shelter. Hedgehogs illustrate perfectly the need for wildlife corridors linking different green areas in towns. When they are searching for food at night, they wander far and wide, and if their travels take them across busy roads they far too often end up squashed.

When most people think of wildlife, they do not immediately think of insects and grubs but of whatever animal or bird they are seeking to encourage. Yet you must first attract the insects and invertebrates that are the food of so many of these other creatures. Unfortunately these include many classified as pests. But do not panic, instead sit back and hope the pest controllers appear soon after the pests. Even slugs become welcome when you see toads, hedgehogs, slow worms or ponderous ground beetles feeding off them, and you will be thankful you have some snails as you watch a thrush crushing their shell on a special stone before devouring the soft parts. Then the sacrifice of a few vegetables and some nibbled foliage becomes somehow less important.

Opposite page: A mature woodland edge in spring; horse chestnut towers above lilac and a beech hedge with wildflowers beneath.

Aphids have probably had the worst press of all. Their presence can turn some gardeners positively neurotic, providing the pesticide industry with millions of pounds as they buy numerous sprays in their attempts to outwit them. You may never see the ladybird or hoverfly larvae hoovering aphids up in droves, but it is a heart-warming sight to watch a sparrow delicately swaying on the stem of a rose as he devours one, or following the ladybirds flying in for a feast. You may learn to identify the many different types of predatory wasps that prey on aphids or lay their eggs in the caterpillars of the white butterflies that descend on your cabbages.

Results will be even better if you take positive action and plant a good variety of attractant plants as well as providing shelter and water. A good pond is the focal point of any wildlife garden. It acts as a place where birds and mammals can drink and feed, where amphibians breed, feed and sunbathe, and where numerous insects can live or visit. Ponds make a real refuge for wetland insects and amphibians.

Birds must be among the most joyful and entertaining of garden visitors and residents. Nothing beats gardening with a cheery robin for company, and they are easily enticed to stay and breed in any garden that provides shelter, food and water. Hedges, trees and shrubberies are invaluable for shelter and nesting opportunities; just make sure they consist of largely native plants, which will then also support plenty of insects to feed the insect-eating birds, and prolific seed, fruit and berry-producing varieties will help the rest. Encourage birds to stay by providing regular food throughout the cold winter months and nesting boxes in sheltered places.

As I sit at my desk writing this, I can see a bullfinch, chaffinch and robin perched on the hazel tree 5 metres/16 feet from my window. Flurries of hedge sparrows are flitting in and out of the brambles and ivy covering the field boundary wall, two blackbirds are pecking at the last of the windfalls from an old apple tree, and a wren is scurrying around in the undergrowth beneath the privet hedge, where bluetits are sheltering. Another robin is in his favourite place, spending many hours seeking out insects among the pile of old stone roofing tiles in front of my office window. I cannot see the birdtable or feeders from here – they became too distracting – but a greater spotted woodpecker, bluetits, nuthatches and greenfinches are among the most regular visitors.

When birds nest, they not only require a safe site, but a territory from which to draw food to feed their young. This is likely to be a much greater area than one garden alone, and the more suitable the network of habitats, the higher the density of nesting birds. Remember that you are not gardening in isolation, and if you encourage neighbours to install bird feeders and plant suitable food and shelter plants, you are doubling up on your chances of hosting a wide range of birds.

Every gardener loves butterflies, the ephemeral angels of the air, and many butterflies have had a particularly lean time due to habitat loss. While most moths can survive in gardens alone given the right attractant plants, butterflies are particularly dependent on specific habitats and maintenance regimes. Gatekeepers and meadow browns will be attracted to wildflower lawns and meadows, but they need a fairly large patch of native grasses if they are to stay and lay their eggs.

You need a large country garden with a carefully maintained meadow if you have any hope of attracting the rare adonis blue and silver-spotted skipper, and species such as the comma and speckled wood butterflies will only be tempted if you have a woodland edge or hedge habitat as they do not fly far and these are their main breeding habitats. Many woodland butterflies require sunny clearings and thrived under the traditional woodland management of coppicing. You are now unlikely to spot high browns, pearl-bordered and heath fritillaries, however if you have a generous woodland edge habitat you may be lucky.

Butterflies are thirsty creatures, and a well-watered garden will be particularly attractive in dry seasons. Water should be from a rainwater butt whenever possible – water conservation is one of the principles of wildlife gardening, which aims to be as sustainable as possible.

Fortunately it is easy to encourage the commoner members of the species – whites, small tortoiseshells, red admirals and peacocks – by providing a sunny border full of nectar-filled plants, early and late flowering plants. Include the ever popular buddleia, and somewhere cosy for tortoiseshells and peacocks to hibernate. Orange tips, painted ladies and brimstones will come to bright nectar-filled flowers whether they are in borders or on balconies, and wildflower lawns attract many species.

The holly blue is a particularly delightful bright blue, looking like a piece of sky flying around the garden. It is easy to cater for as it feeds off holly and ivy. Its numbers fluctuate but it seems to be happy even in urban gardens. Do not fret if predacious wasps descend and attack holly blue caterpillars, if their numbers were not kept down it is likely that some years they could destroy entire holly or ivy plants. Wildlife gardening is about balance, and if you give nature a chance things will usually work out.

This book is above all about gardening with nature to encourage the healthy, beautiful and diverse gardens we are all looking for. Wildlife gardening is not necessarily an easy choice, it requires commitment and patience, but once you have started down the wildlife gardening route, you can be sure you will never turn back. Get out there and enjoy making a difference!

1 First principles

All too often people are put off the idea of gardening for wildlife because they assume it demands a wild garden, with tangled undergrowth and weeds as necessities. This is emphatically not true. A wildlife garden can be every bit as beautiful as a garden planned without wildlife in mind, and it does not have to be untidy.

By definition a garden is not a natural habitat, since any gardening disturbs the balance of nature. The secret of gardening for wildlife lies in tipping this balance in favour of wildlife, while maintaining a garden that works for you. The best wildlife gardens are well managed gardens, just like any other, they are not places where nature has been allowed to take over.

When making any changes to your garden, you need to look at the needs of all the users – and that means humans as well as wildlife. Some people do opt for a slightly overgrown wildlife garden, but others prefer a more formal plan, choosing species and features with care, or allowing one or two areas to have their head. There is no point in changing your garden from a very tidy place to somewhere largely wild if you are very neat by nature and fret at a bit of unkemptness.

If you have a very large garden you can leave some spaces to fend for themselves, without spoiling the overall look. Just wait and see what happens, what new species colonise these set aside areas and which creatures follow. This non-interventionist approach is arguably more about conservation and naturalism than wildlife gardening. People are not involved, which is a shame as part of the joy of gardening for wildlife comes from actively creating a garden where humans and wild creatures can coexist and interact.

It cannot be stressed often enough that it is a myth that a garden should be wild to attract wildlife – you will find more creatures in a well managed garden with a diverse range of plants and habitats than you ever will in a bit of scrubby wilderness. In fact a garden that is neglected will soon become dominated by a few very aggressive species, with a carpet of weeds, thickets of brambles and scruffy woodland springing up. While this will inevitably provide a good place for some creatures – you may get rabbits or foxes and you should get a good range of birds and plenty of insects – a garden designed with wildlife in mind will offer more to a far wider variety of creatures.

Wildlife have simple needs: food, water, shelter and somewhere to breed. Essentially, wildlife gardening means fulfilling these needs, and even small steps can

make a huge difference. So while not every gardener has the space to provide the shelter and cover needed for the widest range of creatures to take up permanent residence and breed, we can all provide something as simple as water for drinking and bathing, and some sources of food.

Your garden is just one of a vast network of gardens across the country, and any steps that you take add an important piece to the overall jigsaw. All forms of wildlife need stopping off points, cafés and watering holes to refuel and refresh themselves, as well as permanent residences where they can shelter and breed.

Flowers, shrubs and trees offer pollen, nectar and seeds; berries and fruit will feed birds, insects, invertebrates and small mammals, and these in turn are the food for other insects, birds and mammals. Similarly plant debris and animal droppings rotting on the ground feed ground-living and soil-dwelling insects and micro-organisms, which then feed the soil that feeds the plants that feed the wildlife… and so on. Please note, however, that the one garnish you must never add to the basic range of wildlife food is chemicals.

Styles of gardening

Making a garden wildlife-friendly means providing habitats that mimic those in nature and complement the local range outside the garden. The best advice for anyone wanting to start a wildlife garden is simply to dig a pond, plant some hardy perennials and let a few native wildflowers and weeds grow, then birds, bees, insects and frogs will appear as if by magic. If this is all you ever do, you will have made a difference, but chances are that before long you will want to extend the habitats and encourage more creatures to share your outdoor space. The basic principle of wildlife gardening is to design and manage your garden with the specific purpose of creating diversity.

Most new wildlife gardeners will be enhancing or converting existing gardens, rather than starting from scratch. Instead of making dramatic changes straight away, there are plenty of small steps you can take that will make a significant difference to the range of creatures your garden attracts and supports. If you want more birds, for example, simply add a birdbath and some feeding stations. Of course if you want them to stay and breed you will need to make sure your garden offers adequate shelter and protection, as well as a good source of food.

You do not have to get there in one step, it can be a gradual process, starting with a few basic but effective changes. For example, a simple alteration to garden management, such as leaving plant debris on the beds rather than raking it away in autumn, can make

Above: Old-fashioned cottage garden plants are particularly popular with butterflies, bees and insects.

Opposite page: A shallow pond attracts amphibians and aquatic insects and allows a gardener to introduce a different range of plants.

**CHECKLIST
WILDLIFE-FRIENDLY
FEATURES**

Native plants

Native species of plants – from tiny flowers to huge trees – host many more species of insects and caterpillars than non-native, as our native fauna has evolved along with our native flora.

Water

A pond brings masses of creatures to drink as well as attracting resident pond life, including frogs, toads, newts, diving beetles and dragonflies, possibly even water voles.

Wildflowers, grasses and weeds

Wildflowers and native grasses attract butterflies and many other insects, including grasshoppers. Nettles are among the important weeds that host species important to the health of your garden. If you do not want a patch of nettles, be generous and grow a container full especially for butterflies and ladybirds.

Nectar and pollen-rich flowering plants

Flowers provide nectar and pollen to feed butterflies, bees, hoverflies and numerous other insects that act as pollinators and pest controllers in your garden; they also attract birds.

Opposite page: Camassias, clovers, buttercups and daisies in an early summer meadow.

a huge difference. You will probably scarcely notice any difference in the way your garden looks, but many small creatures and birds will appreciate the gesture.

The traditional cottage garden is a pretty ideal wildlife garden. It typically has an abundance of flowering plants from early spring until late in the autumn, there are usually rambling climbers and scented plants, a hedge, quite often a pond or other source of water, and a fruit tree or two. There also tends to be a productive kitchen garden where flowers are allowed to spread and grow among the vegetables, and fertiliser is provided by compost and muck – no chemicals. All this bounty provides an abundance of food, as well as homes and shelter, and as a result cottage gardens are usually alive with birds and insects, as well as more secretive creatures.

Permaculture is another style of gardening that can provide maximum opportunities for wildlife. This is a system of gardening where several layers of plants are grown in productive layers one above the other, providing maximum productivity in minimum space with no chemical inputs. Permaculture provides flowerbeds, orchard, kitchen garden and woodland edge habitats all in one, and can offer wonderful diversity for wildlife if predominantly native species are used. Of course this method is not to everyone's taste. Permaculture gardens are planned with diversity and productivity in mind, where plants support each other as much as possible so inputs are minimal and outputs are maximum; they are often criticised for being less than aesthetically pleasing to someone used to looking at more conventional gardens. But beauty is in the eye of the beholder, and it can be a very joyous sight to see a packed garden overflowing with fruit and berries, crawling with insects, clouded with butterflies and alive with birds.

If your preference is for something rather more formal, you do not have to change your style completely to make your garden more friendly for wildlife. If you have clipped hedges, choose species that wildlife appreciate, and when choosing plants for your borders think about the specific varieties that insects and butterflies love. A formal pond can be wildlife friendly if you add stones for accessibility.

Even if you pride yourself on a closely cropped lawn, do consider leaving an area of less well-tended grass somewhere in your garden – a smooth green sward will not support anything except a lawnmower. An attractive and tidy alternative to a conventional lawn is to sow or plant meadow flowers in your grass: cowslips, yarrow, Lady's smock, yellow rattle and self-heal usually establish easily, depending on your soil type, and they are useful host, food and nectar plants for a range of insects and butterflies.

Simpler still is to leave one patch of grass to grow slightly wild or keep it rough, you may be surprised at the diversity of grasses, mosses, wildflowers and weed plants that

will appear of their own accord. In a former garden I had a badly drained, rather stony patch of rough grass beside the drive, where roots struggled to take hold in thin earth above sand and rubble; weeds loved it, fungi flourished and only the toughest grass grew, but I will never forget looking out of an upstairs window early one summer morning and seeing a whole family of green woodpeckers, both parents and four offspring, pecking merrily away, feeding on the ants that colonised the patch. Even my non-garden minded teenage son was impressed when I woke him up to watch. That was so much more interesting than another conventional patch of lawn.

Native plants and natural habitats

One question that is often raised about wildlife gardening is the importance of native species. Wildlife gardening does not mean you have to restrict yourself purely to native plants, but it does mean you should plant as many as possible. Generally, native British species will be at home in British gardens and will support more wildlife than exotics, because over time the plants have developed relationships with each other or with native wildlife and fungi, as well as adapting themselves to withstand our climate and conditions.

Many insects are totally specific about their food, with their larvae relying on the leaves of one particular native species. Insects must be encouraged as they are the backbone of any wildlife garden – being food for so many carnivorous insects, birds, bats and small mammals. Some birds also need the fruit and seeds of natives.

But it is not quite as cut-and-dried as this. Just because something is native to the UK does not mean it will necessarily grow well in your soil or area. In fact some true natives are not ideal for usually fertile garden conditions, while, conversely, imported species can be easy to maintain and can provide excellent wildlife shelter and food. There are circumstances where exotics do fit the bill as well if not better than natives: for example buddleia is one of the very best butterfly plants, nicotiana (tobacco plant) is superb for moths, wisteria provides excellent cover and food, and berried plants such as cotoneasters and pyracanthas can be very good value, providing shelter as well as food.

Scented herbs are invaluable, and many non-native, colourful border plants are indispensable – especially at the end of season when plants such as *Verbena bonariensis* provide late food for butterflies. If you only have room for one or two trees, you must go native (see chapter eight), but if you have room for more, you can expand your horizons. Borders should include as many types of herbaceous plants as possible for diversity, a herb patch growing only natives would be impoverished for wildlife and humans alike. As long as you include a range of native plants, you do not need to feel too restricted.

Above: *Verbena bonariensis* is a favourite late summer food for butterflies.

Opposite page: The red berries of pyracantha attracts dozens of birds.

**CHECKLIST
WILDLIFE-FRIENDLY
FEATURES**

**Trees, flowering and
fruiting shrubs**
Birds need food and shelter, give
them an insect-rich native tree or
two, berrying and fruiting plants
and shrubby cover.

Climbing plants
Cover for birds, food for insects
and butterflies.

Hedges
Fruiting and flowering hedges
provide food and shelter for
wildlife, nesting places for birds
and cover for hedgehogs, voles
and shrews.

Wood pile
Insects colonise decaying wood,
attracting spiders and birds. Stag
beetles and other beetles lay their
grubs in rotting wood. Toads and
hedgehogs may hibernate
underneath it, and slow worms
(which prey on slugs) may use it
as home.

Compost heap
Provides food for the soil and a
home for tiny insects and mini
beasts which feed birds,
hedgehogs and toads. Hedgehogs,
toads and slow worms may nest
in the centre.

Another, related question, is the advisability of creating mini-habitats that do not follow the natural ecology of your area. Some habitats can be easily recreated even if they are not the dominant ecology in your locality, but if you are going against your local flora, remember that it will be difficult for wildlife to colonise your garden unless there are sufficient wildlife corridors in the vicinity linking similar habitats. An isolated patch of chalk grassland, for example, in an area of predominantly acid habitats, can provide a haven for some creatures, but it will provide the best wildlife value if there is a network of similar habitats within reach for flying, crawling or wandering creatures.

However, a chalky grassland is a very diverse habitat, and one of the easiest to recreate. It may be the ideal environment for a brand new garden where the soil is little more than builders' rubble, and is also quite easy to create in a derelict site, or following demolition or building work. You need to build a very alkaline base and cover it thoroughly with about 10cm/4in of topsoil, and while you can import chalk or crushed limestone, a base of crushed cement and rubble will work just as well. It is more difficult to create an acid environment without importing quantities of peaty soil and subsoil from a genuine habitat, which is only desirable if such a habitat is being destroyed for road-building or other development.

You will have to work very hard to turn an alien habitat into a wildlife haven as there will be little else nearby to support and entice the insects and other creatures that appreciate that particular environment, and you will not enjoy a diverse spread of plants because there will be nowhere for them to spread from. It is better to create habitats that can be supported by and supportive of their surroundings.

However much you dream of creating a seaside habitat with appropriate planting and landscaping, if you live inland the only real way to create a maritime garden is to move to the sea. But it can still be fun to create some foreign environments in your garden and see what plants and creatures spring up in them, and how they survive or flourish. So if you really feel the urge, then have a go. Just remember that although these experiments may have some wildlife value, these will always be limited as such an out-of-place environment can never be sustainable. And above all, wildlife gardening should be sustainable. It should encourage the natural spread of communities of plants and creatures, which means whenever possible you must try and mesh with the local ecology and landscape.

Providing food

An ideal wildlife larder contains a broad mixture of flowering and fruiting plants, starting with bulbs in early spring and leaving some perennials to run to seed for

autumn and winter food, along with fruiting trees and shrubs. Cottage garden style flowers and aromatic plants appeal to wildlife as much as to gardeners. Wildflowers are important, and many – such as knapweed, cornflowers, poppies, chicory and varieties of bellflowers – are excellent border plants. Herbs attract insects, and night scented flowers attract moths and other night flying insects that are important to bats and other night-time feeders.

All but the most sterile garden will already provide some or all of these foodstuffs, after all most gardens have flowerbeds, or flowering plants in containers, their nectar and pollen the staple diet for many creatures, their seeds food for later in the year. Many gardens also have shrubs, trees and hedges with a broader mix of flowers and fruits. It adds another dimension to gardening to choose plants for their wildlife value as well as their colour, shape and habit.

It is particularly important to think of providing food in winter, and even the most abundantly planted garden may need to install a few bird feeders for extra help over these lean months. Just be selective, as over-provision can encourage all the squabbling greedy neighbourhood magpies and pigeons at the expense of the more timid finches, tits and smaller birds.

Food does not just mean sustenance for herbivores, you must also provide for carnivorous appetites, and insects make up the staple diet for hundreds of other insects, birds and small mammals, which in turn may be the chosen dish of larger mammals. So you need to grow the right plants to host insects – even those that you might think of as pests, such as aphids – as these then become food for creatures on the next step of the food chain.

Gardeners new to wildlife gardening often find it pretty difficult to turn a blind eye to aphids or slugs, as most will have spent years doing all they can to eradicate them. But it is really important to cultivate a relaxed attitude to signs of the insects you think of as pests. They have a role to play as food for other creatures that you want to encourage. Your garden will recover faster and be much healthier in the long run if you can re-establish the natural balance of pest and predator. Of course it may look a bit tatty round the edges while it is reclaiming this balance. Do not give up. With your help this balance will return and eventually you will stop worrying about the occasional munched or yellowing leaf or bud.

Chemicals

Wildlife and chemicals do not mix. Over the past fifty years we have been bombarded with an ever more sophisticated barrage of possible chemical weapons. Magazines advertise pest sprays for every conceivable species of bug, there are dozens of substances to combat specific pests as well as general multipurpose killers, there are potions to combat all manner of diseases and we are offered weedkillers for every type of weed, as well as specifics to rout particular offenders.

If you are used to using chemicals and having a glossy garden full of perfect blooms it takes a great effort of will not to rush out and attack when pests seem to be munching their way through your plants. Similarly when weeds are trying to take over or the telltale signs of disease appear, the temptation to reach for the spray can seem overwhelming. But if you keep spraying, you will never solve the problem. All you are doing is spending money to make your situation worse.

A garden is a perfect illustration of the web of life and the interdependence of different organisms. Probably the crucial difference between conventional gardening and wildlife gardening is that practitioners have to think like ecologists, as well as gardeners, and recognise how many actions can have effects further along the chain.

If you think about the food chain and the fact that smaller creatures feed bigger creatures, you will understand that if you want to attract other forms of wildlife into the garden, encourage insects. Looking after the bottom links in the chain by

Opposite page: A thrush will return to the same stone to de-shell snails.

providing habitats for insects and invertebrates ensures plenty of their predators will turn up to eat them. Plant-feeding insects, for example, are a source of food for a wide range of carnivores, including spiders, centipedes, ground beetles, dragonflies, amphibians, bats, reptiles, moles, hedgehogs, foxes and badgers, as well as birds. These carnivores also feed off the small scavengers that live off decaying materials – insects, grubs, woodlice, worms, snails and slugs. The more food you provide, the more creatures you attract.

Spraying against insect pests is the worst action any gardener can take, as every bug is potential food for another creature. So when you spray you not only kill the pests, but also their natural predators. It is all to do with the interdependence of living things. Aphids, for example, are food for ladybirds, lacewings and hoverflies, and when you spray the aphids you will also kill the creatures that are eating them. On top of that, aphids breed faster than their predators, so the next generation of bugs will have no natural controls, and so the aphid problem will get worse and you will probably keep spraying because you have obliterated the natural remedy.

On the other hand, if you grit your teeth and resist the urge to spray at the first sight of aphids colonising your plants, after a few days the predators will move in. Then if you look closely at aphid infested plants you will also see lots of tiny greyish-brown alligator-like creatures among the aphid colonies. These are the larvae of ladybirds or hoverflies piercing hundreds of aphids an hour and sucking out their juice, and when the adults hatch they will continue the job. The balance is not always perfect, but you can also distract the pests and attract predators with judicious planting and garden management.

Another problem with chemical killers is that some creatures that you would welcome in your garden may prey upon poisoned carcasses – when thrushes and hedgehogs eat poisoned slugs, for example, it can poison them too. Chemical weed control is equally unhelpful; when you spray weeds you introduce toxins to the soil and destroy the micro-organisms, invertebrates and bacteria that keep the soil healthy, allowing it to nourish plants and, therefore, other creatures. You kill the weeds, but you also kill the soil, which then needs building up with all sorts of fertilisers in order to support plants.

Another danger is that you may also kill the source of food for many creatures you want in your garden – such as various species of butterfly. If everyone sprayed nettles, for example, we would be much the poorer: nettles are host plants for early aphids that feed ladybirds and other helpful insects, which are the food for the caterpillars of several butterflies. Without them we would have no red admirals, peacocks or small

tortoiseshells, and commas would struggle. Nettles also do a good job out of sight, for below the ground their roots mine for minerals and help increase fertility, which adds to the diversity of soil life, which again attracts more creatures.

Water and shelter

Every garden needs water, for creatures to drink and bathe in – and to encourage wetland wildlife. Adding some kind of water feature to a garden is probably the quickest way to encourage wildlife to move in. Within hours of filling an old sink with water you may find that pond-skaters or water boatmen have arrived, and frogs will soon find their way to your water if there is some shady damp vegetation nearby – frog numbers have slumped dramatically in the countryside over the past twenty years but risen overall, thanks to the vast increase in garden ponds. Dragonflies and other insects also often appear promptly if you put your sink in a sunny spot, and many insects start

Above: Decaying logs in a sheltered place provide homes for beetles and insects and sometimes for small mammals and amphibians.

their lives in water. Then there are all the visitors who come to drink, from birds and flying insects to crawling and scuttling creatures.

Even a birdbath makes a big difference to the variety of birds you will attract, as well as creatures coming to drink. A birdbath does not have to be elaborate, birds are quite happy with an upturned dustbin lid sunk into the edge of a flowerbed or path – but if your garden is also home to cats make sure you raise the container off the ground and place it well away from cover where cats could lie in wait. A birdbath is not a luxury but a necessity for many birds, and it is particularly important to keep it unfrozen in winter as they need to bathe to keep their plumage in good condition to withstand harsh weather.

Shelter is the major consideration if you want creatures to make their home in your garden rather than simply using it as a rest stop. Insects need stones and plants to crawl under or soil to burrow into; a bit of rotting vegetation is ideal and good ground cover planting or a mulch of any sort shelters beetles and all sorts of crawling insects, while flying insects will burrow into moist soil or nooks and crannies in bark, walls and logs. Dry stone walls provide lots of opportunities for insects and even small mammals to hide in, and butterflies may crawl into the cracks in sunny walls to hibernate. Walls and stones are also favourite places for slugs and snails to curl up.

An excellent way of encouraging insects, woodlice, spiders, mites and beetles is to leave a pile or two of old logs somewhere in your garden. They really appreciate the damp conditions provided by rotting wood, especially behind peeling bark. If you baulk at the idea of having rotting wood lying around, you can hide a log or two in a shady hidden corner or behind a shed, the insects will not mind.

Drier parts of a wood pile may provide homes for the small tortoiseshell, large tortoiseshell and comma butterflies to hibernate, and a wood shed or other outbuilding with easy access points will also provide alternative winter quarters for butterflies. Hordes of ladybirds may also take up winter residence in a wood pile, or in old wooden posts. Bumblebees may make their nests under dry sheds, or buried in a dry bank.

Birds need the cover and protection of thick vegetation, ideally in shrubs, hedges or tangled climbing plants, and coniferous trees can also offer very good nesting opportunities. If birds are going to breed in your garden, they need sources of food and material for nest-building – housemartins, for example, need mud, so are most likely to make their homes near a pond or wetland. As they also like some privacy, they look for quiet spots.

Birds and bats need to be safe from the attention of cats. You can help by putting up bird and bat boxes, but remember that they will not be much good on their own if

**CHECKLIST
WILDLIFE-FRIENDLY
FEATURES**

Bird and bat boxes
Put up nesting and roosting boxes in secluded and sheltered parts of your garden for birds and bats.

Bird table and bird feeders
However considerately your garden is planted, birds need extra food in winter.

Birdbath
Birds need somewhere to bathe to keep their plumage in good condition throughout the year. Keep it unfrozen in winter.

Stones and walls
Toads, newts and female frogs usually spend winter on land, under rockery stones (or in a log pile). Beetles, spiders and other insects live in the nooks and crannies.

NEVER USE pesticides, herbicides or slug pellets or you will kill off species which are links in the food chain.

Opposite page: Frogs need damp vegetation for shelter as well as water for breeding.

your garden does not also provide food, water and some cover. Nothing is going to want to make its home in a box on a bare wall without any leafy cover – if creatures are going to breed in your garden they need places to hide. The larger the garden, the larger the range of nooks and crannies there is likely to be, places where creatures can hide away undisturbed. However even a tiny tidy garden can afford excellent shelter for birds and small mammals, as long as there are a few climbers.

Ivy gets a generally bad press, condemned for pulling out mortar and burrowing into walls allowing damp to seep in and cause decay. However this reputation is really undeserved. Of course ivy's suckering habit will put pressure on already weak mortar, but if your walls are in good condition it will cause no harm, acting instead as a layer of insulation and providing dense coverage, generous pollen and places for birds, such as wrens, to nest. Ivy also has the great advantage of growing happily and fast in shade and on cold walls.

Honeysuckle and quince are inviting for birds and butterflies, and many birds love to nest in the tangled stems of wisteria and clematis. When you plant climbers that need to be tied into a framework, place any supports several inches away from the wall to allow for a wildlife corridor between plant and wall.

Small mammals need logs, old pipes, walls or leafy undergrowth for quiet hiding places. You can help some animals, for example hedgehogs, by providing boxes where they can make their homes, but these must be camouflaged and placed in a quiet place as wild creatures are naturally shy. Aquatic creatures need damp vegetation, although toads and frogs are quite versatile and happily live under upturned flowerpots or damp stones. However they will not stay in your garden, even if it has a pond, if there is nowhere to hide or hunt. Larger mammals need space to make their dens.

Few of us can provide varied enough habitats to accommodate all the wildlife we might like, and even if we do provide the perfect places, it does not always mean that the creatures you expect will automatically move in. Yet any steps you make are worth taking. You might never be able to provide a diverse enough habitat to support the whole life cycle of a particular creature, but you may be able to provide a place where they can forage. If you have not got the space for a hedge, you may be able to plant climbing plants that offer similar possibilities. If you cannot run to a wildflower meadow, a few wildflowers in a trough or a window box can attract hundreds of insects all summer long.

Do not ever be discouraged. Even if your contribution seems very small, it really can make a difference. The patchwork of tiny gardens, balconies, roof gardens and even hanging baskets dotted around our cities are vitally important. Together they make up invaluable wildlife corridors, places where wildlife can travel safely in search of hospitality, being fed and watered along the journey. A hanging basket full of bright nectar-rich flowers in a concrete jungle really could make the difference between a butterfly's survival and death. The potential knock-on effects are huge.

Links between gardens are crucial, so if you have the opportunity, plant a hedge rather than erecting a fence, grow some shrubs, keep an area of long grass, let intertwining climbers ramble over boundaries. Within a garden you need to create links between different areas along which small mammals and invertebrates can scuttle happily. Even if you choose very wildlife-friendly plants, you are going to have a hard job persuading many creatures to head for a totally exposed flowerbed, container or tree in the middle of a patch of shorn grass or hard paving. Hedging is invaluable if you have the space and situation, otherwise group shrubs or even containers together, provide some shade and shelter around a flowerbed, and plant some cover beside large expanses of paving.

Welcoming all visitors

One factor that puts some people off wildlife gardening is the thought that the measures you take will encourage all wildlife, even some creatures that you consider pests. No-one wants rats in their gardens, for example, and it is important to discourage them with good practice, such as keeping the area around a bird table clear of old food scraps and being careful about what you put in your compost. Moles can be rather unwelcome, particularly in the vegetable patch – although molehill soil makes very fine compost – and only the largest gardens want to host a badgers' sett or foxes' den.

Badgers are gardeners' friends in that they eat slugs, snails and earwigs, but they also eat young hedgehogs, they love earthworms, and are persistent diggers, clawing up tufts of grass and plants to get at the roots or invertebrates beneath. They thrive in the area around where I live and though I love to see them making their way around the countryside in the evenings, I confess that I try to keep them out of the garden as I find their persistent digging rather irritating. I would also prefer it if rabbits kept away because of their fondness for young shoots and plants, but I have found that by barricading specific areas we can tolerate each other.

The decision to create and maintain a wildlife-friendly garden is to cultivate a relaxed attitude to gardening and to learn to give and take. If birds strip too many of your fruit bushes you can always net the fruit, if your vegetables prove irresistible to winged and furry creatures, protect them to ensure you get your fair share. The joy of seeing new visitors take up residence in your garden will, I promise, be worth it.

2 Garden management

Opposite page: Standing seedheads look stunning in winter, and provide food for hungry birds.

From the start, gardens have many potential advantages for wildlife over the so-called natural habitats of the countryside. They can have much wider diversity in a small area than any piece of countryside, and they often offer excellent shelter and much greater supplies of food than is usually available in the wild. One garden typically contains a number of different habitats, with trees, shrubs, grassland, bare soil, flowerbeds, paved areas, compost heaps, wood piles, walls and often a pond. There is usually a large diversity of plants. Additionally, gardens are more intensively managed than most areas of countryside, and although this can mean disturbance, it also brings plenty of benefits, such as a constant supply of new foliage that comes from regular sowing and planting, pruning and cutting.

Although a garden is not a natural habitat, or series of habitats, it can still operate as an ecosystem, with species all interacting to support each other, and additionally with interaction with neighbouring gardens and planted areas. This sustainable ideal is the aim for any wildlife gardener, and can be realised by following general techniques to establish and maintain habitats as well as good practice.

Knowing your garden

Soil and the plants and wildlife it supports varies from area to area, and different types need different care. A patch of chalk grassland has hugely different needs from a patch of lowland heath, and a damp woodland habitat requires different management from a fertile border. However the principles remain the same – look after the basics and the plants will look after themselves. Healthy plants attract a variety of wildlife, which in turn attracts more. Wildlife gardening is a branch of organic gardening, co-operating with nature rather than battling against it. To be successful at making and maintaining garden habitats – especially in a small space – you need to understand environmentally friendly gardening practices.

The foundation of all conventional gardening practice is to build up and maintain healthy soil, which will keep your plants free from diseases and resistant to pests. In nature plants adapt to their particular conditions, with different plants thriving in different types of soils, so if you understand how soil works you can help nature overcome most restrictions and build a wide range of healthy habitats.

One big difference in wildlife gardening from a more traditional approach is that you can choose to leave some patches of thin or heavy soil, rather than improving the

SEASONAL TASKS

January
Order seeds.
Keep water ice free.
Care for the birds.
Position bat boxes.

February
Site nesting boxes.
Feed the birds.
Prune buddleia and overgrown
shrubs.
Prune native fruiting and
berrying hedges.

March
Clear autumn mulch off beds.
Cultivate, but not when soil is wet.
Divide established marginal,
pond and wetland plants.
Plant snowdrops.
Divide congested herbaceous
plants and trim back other
perennials.

April
Sow hardy annuals and
wildflower mixtures as weather
improves.
Mow wildflower meadows sown
the previous autumn.
Plant water and wetland plants.
Mulch borders.

May
Plant out half hardy annuals.
Prune woody spring flowering
shrubs.

fertility of all of your garden. This is because the plants that colonise rough ground attract a different class of visitor to those growing in more fertile areas. Of course good fertile soil supports the widest range of plants, so aim to build and maintain fertility. Even if your soil starts off thin, stony and dusty, or heavy, wet and muddy, with time and good practice you will be able to build it up so that you can grow the widest range of plants for the greatest diversity of wildlife.

Your garden soil depends to some extent on your location, rainfall and aspect – how much sun you get in different parts of the garden – but it also reflects the local ecology, and its quality will depend on how the garden has been managed in the past. Plants need air, sunlight and water, but they also need chemical elements from the soil. Whether your soil is acid or alkaline will depend on how easy it is for plants to take up these nutrients from the soil, and the structure of your soil will determine how you work it to make these elements more available.

Nitrogen, phosphorous and potassium are the most important; magnesium, calcium and sulphur are essential, and plants also need trace elements. Some elements become locked up in acid soils, and some are not available in alkaline soils, so you need to know whether your soil is acid or alkaline. Acidity and alkalinity is measured on a pH scale, which runs from 1 to 14 with neutral at 6.5 to 7.0. Anything below is acid (strongly acid would be a peat bog environment), anything above 7.5 to 8.0 is alkaline (such as chalk downland).

You can affect the pH by adding soil improvers, such as garden compost, but you also need to work with it, growing plants that are appropriate. You cannot grow acid-loving plants, such as heathers, in alkaline soil, and wildflowers such as fritillaries, will not tolerate acid conditions. You also need to work with the texture of your soil, which directly affects its capacity to retain moisture and nutrients as well as its ability to make them available to plants.

Gardeners with new homes are generally considered at a great disadvantage, because the soil is often thin, stony and heavily compacted, or it may consist of little more than subsoil. It takes determination to turn this into rich fertile soil, but it can be useful for some habitats. Wildflowers, for example, prefer very poor soil, and will not thank you for improving the fertility of the ground. Similarly, new ponds should be lined with at least 10cm/4in of very infertile soil as a base for aquatic plants – anything more fertile encourages algae. Some insects thrive in badly drained compacted soil, and they may attract other creatures. Ants, for example, are extremely undesirable in the vegetable patch where they will steal seeds and prevent germination, but they are more than acceptable in a patch of poor grass on rough soil, where they are targets for woodpeckers and other birds.

Fertile soil encourages the greatest diversity of plant life, and all the other life forms that go with it. Building fertility means adding organic matter to your soil; it is never a good plan to add synthetic fertilisers or chemical quick-fixes as these can destroy many of the soil's tiny life forms and lead to long-term problems. Organic matter is the decaying remains of plants and animals, and it provides a source of nitrogen and phosphorus which is essential to healthy plant growth, along with all the other necessary minerals and trace elements. Organic matter includes garden compost and manure, rotted leaves and woodchips, which will decay into the rich humus that keeps your soil healthy.

Most gardens have slight variations in the texture of the soil, depending on the way the garden has been managed. The most manageable garden soil is crumbly loam, where the particles stick together in an assortment of large and small crumbs. This is the ideal, but it usually takes some work to get there. Often gardens have patches of rich loamy soil, usually where vegetables have been grown and heaps of organic matter have been incorporated over years, but there are usually also troublespots.

In light sandy soils large particles refuse to join together, so air and water along with nutrients drain very swiftly through them. At the other end of the scale, in heavy clay soils the particles are so tiny that they cling together in sticky clods, stopping air and water from finding a way through. Incorporating garden compost corrects both problems, lightening and aerating a heavy soil and making a light one more spongy and absorbent.

One of the wonderful things about compost is that it works with the soil to release nutrients gradually through the growing season when plants need them most. When soil is cool – when plants are young in spring, or slowing down for winter – compost releases nutrients slowly, but as soil temperatures heat up and plants move into a stage of more rapid growth, the decomposers in the compost and the soil work harder and release more plant food.

If you have a particularly waterlogged area, the usual advice is to lay land drains to improve the drainage. However, instead of following conventional wisdom, follow one of the main tenets of wildlife gardening and work with nature rather than battling against it. Do not think of this area as a troublespot, instead turn it to your advantage and leave it as a boggy patch. This will be a boon to your wildlife garden, as it will soon develop into a flourishing habitat that will be home to a whole range of creatures that you would not find elsewhere in your garden.

SEASONAL TASKS

June
Cut down your nettle patch by half to provide new growth for egg-laying butterflies.
Mow spring wildflower lawns.

July
Cut out stems of rambling roses that have finished flowering.
Deadhead flowers to encourage continuous flowering.

August
Keep birdbaths and ponds regularly topped up.
Plant autumn flowering bulbs.
Collect wildflower seed.
Deadhead buddleia to encourage it to continue flowering into the autumn; it is an important nectar plant for late butterflies.
Trim evergreen hedges.
Prune deciduous non-fruiting hedges once nesting birds have vacated.

The compost heap

Every garden needs its soil life, from worms to tiny bacteria, and every wildlife garden should have a compost heap or bin, for the good of the soil and for the creatures it offers a home to. Adding compost to your soil improves its structure and builds it into the ideal condition to accept and use nutrients effectively. It also adds those nutrients, returning plants and tiny living creatures that came from the soil, back to the soil, in the form of the minerals, proteins, carbohydrates and sugars that plants and animals need to grow.

Organic waste matter is rotted by the action of tiny organisms, and a compost heap is not just a heap of old waste but a teeming pile of life and energy – macro- and micro-organisms, chemical and physical processes, reproduction, death, birth, all life's processes are here. Macro-organisms include all the tiny soil dwellers: mites, centipedes, millipedes, spiders, springtails, beetles, ants, flies, nematodes and earthworms. So a compost heap is not only home for hundreds of insects and invertebrates, it is also a huge feeding station for all sorts of birds and small mammals who prey on the compost workers as they start the job of decomposing material, dragging waste through the heap and chewing, grinding, sucking or tearing it into smaller pieces.

Next the micro-organisms – bacteria and fungi – get to work and digest whatever they come across, liberating nutritious elements locked into the materials. As the bacteria feed on the waste they break down compounds and grow and multiply, releasing heat as they increase, and providing the conditions for different strains of organisms to carry on the work of efficient composting. The warmth also means that a free-standing compost heap can be a snug place for small mammals, amphibians and grass snakes to burrow into and hibernate.

All composting methods are designed to meet the needs of the organisms that do the decomposing. They need a varied diet, including some very fibrous materials and some soft leafy waste, and they need air, moisture and warmth. This means that compost can be made in any container that allows air to flow in and out and that can keep heat and moisture in while keeping cold and rain out. Structures can be temporary or permanent, moveable or fixed. What you choose will largely depend on how much waste you produce in your kitchen and garden, how much space you have and how much compost you need – although you will find that you can never produce enough.

In a small garden you may like to compost in a commercial container, otherwise the easiest and most versatile method of composting is to build a cool heap or make sectioned wooden bins. Any heap – or home-made bin – should be at least 1m/3ft wide, deep and tall. This means it has the best chance of heating up and retaining its heat, while being unlikely to dry out quickly. Much larger heaps can be tricky to manage as

Opposite page: A compost heap is teeming with life – essential for the health of any garden.

Above: Grass snakes may hunt for food in sunny garden ponds.

air may not be able to get to the centre and material will tend to pack down unevenly.

When you start a compost heap try and lay down as large a heap of material as possible at once to give the organisms plenty to get started with. It is a good idea to gather a few bags of garden or kitchen waste over a week or two ready for composting. I prefer to build straight on to the earth to give the soil organisms a chance to help the initial processes, starting with a bit of brushwood for air, but some people put wire mesh at the base, or even build compost bins on to a solid base. It is up to you, just make sure air and moisture can get to the heap.

A good beginning is a layer of grass clippings, then a layer of soft kitchen and garden waste, followed by a thin dry layer of straw, twigs, or paper, and a layer of manure – then start again. But it really is not as crucial as some compost buffs will tell you – everything will decompose given the right conditions, all you need to do is make sure that you provide a fairly varied diet.

There is a lot of rotten advice about the difficulties of composting grass clippings. Take no notice and do not be shy of using them, they are rich in nitrogen and perfect on a compost heap, just do not add too thick a lump of mowings at once, or they will deteriorate into a slimy mat which will stop air getting through. Similarly do not add too thick a bundle or layer of very dry material unless you are topping it with at least an equal volume of soft and easy-to-decompose waste. Otherwise please yourself. Nettles, comfrey and manure help keep the composting process moving along, and urine also speeds up the processes.

It is best to compost autumn leaves separately and use them as a distinct mulch and soil conditioner, and manure should only be added in fairly small quantities. Make a separate muck heap if you have space, otherwise buy it in bags. A compost heap will take around six months to produce useable compost, and it is common to fill one section of a bin and leave it from spring to autumn, while filling the next from spring to autumn ready for use the following spring. Compost takes longer to develop in winter, when the weather is cool.

Peat belongs in bogs

Garden centres still sell peat as a soil improver. Please do not buy it. Peat extraction is responsible for the destruction of particularly fragile habitats which are home to many rare dragonflies, butterflies and birds. Peat develops naturally over a very long period in a living bog. It is formed when plants living on the surface – such as sphagnum mosses, bog cotton and heathers – die. Instead of decomposing as plants would in other environments, the waterlogged ground turns the dead matter into peat.

In Ireland, the main source of peat during the second half of the twentieth century, less than six per cent of their natural peat bogs remain, leaving many bog plants and animals desperately struggling for survival – some have already become extinct. Bog animals and plants need peat, the plants in your garden do not, they will be quite happy with alternatives.

If you are looking for a soil improver to add texture and structure, garden compost and leaf mould are much better than peat, as peat adds very few nutrients to soil. Mulches are very useful in a wildlife garden because they provide a home for all sorts of ground dwelling insects and invertebrates. Peat is also often recommended as a garden mulch to lay on top of the soil to suppress weeds and conserve nutrients and moisture. However, bark products will do the job far better than peat, they are especially good combined with muck and garden compost, or even cocoashells or coconut fibre (coir).

Planting to encourage pest predators

When you have got your soil as it should be, you can get on with planting. There is no reason not to include your favourite ornamentals, but the priority is to plant with wildlife in mind. You need a good range of native plants to provide food and homes for wildlife. Nectar- and pollen-producing flowers, climbers, shrubs, ground cover plants, berrying plants and scented herbs are all ideal. When you are thinking about encouraging wildlife, it cannot be stressed often enough that there is no place for chemicals, so you must think like an ecologist, considering the webs of life that a garden supports, and how best to maintain it.

Some insects are conventionally seen as pests because they eat leaves and buds, damage fruit trees and bark, and generally affect the health and appearance of your plants. Try to cultivate a tolerant attitude to signs of minor pest damage. In fact stop thinking of the insects as pests, and think of them, instead, as meals for other creatures. Remember you are aiming to create a balance, and if you succeed you will have the added bonus of being much less stressed about each nibbled leaf or misshapen bud.

Every garden must be visited regularly by bees and other pollinators, and many of these are also important pest killers. Lacewings are beautiful delicate insects with translucent pale green wings, and greenfly are their favourite food. Hoverflies are like miniature darting wasps, and parasitic wasps are very skinny and narrow-waisted –

Below: Comfrey feeds the soil and provides food for insects.

Opposite page: The attractive pink whorls of water mint are rich in pollen.

Right: Dill and other umbellifers bring hoverflies into the garden.

they lay their eggs in soft-bodied insects, mainly caterpillars, and the hatching grubs then feed on the bodies of their hosts, eventually killing them.

You may never spot some of the most efficient pest controllers of all, tiny larvae which prey on soft-bodied insects, mites and insect eggs. Lacewing larvae look like miniature greenish grey alligators and not only dispose of aphids but also attack caterpillars and insect larvae, piercing their prey and sucking out their juices. One larva can get through more than a hundred aphids in an hour! Brownish green hoverfly larvae do severe damage to aphid colonies, and tiny greyish ladybird larvae are also voracious. Then the adults come along and continue the killing.

It is a bit of a cliché that wildlife gardens should contain patches of nettles, but valuable advice nonetheless. Nettles are important, not only because they are the favoured food of some of our best-loved butterflies, but because they attract aphids as meals for early ladybird and hoverfly larvae, which then move on to feast on insect pests elsewhere. Plant your nettles in a sunny spot, and if you want to keep them under control contain their roots in an old bucket to stop them running. Let them flower, then cut them down before they seed everywhere, and allow them a second chance.

Aphids tend to be plant specific; however, luckily their predators are not so fussy. You often notice numbers of aphids early in the spring, before too many other insects are obvious, so you make sure you have some early flowering scented plants, such as wallflowers, to attract the early pest controllers and pollinators.

Aromatic herbs are popular with all helpful insects, so plant borage, hyssop, sages and lavenders, and mints in pots. A few lavender plants among your roses look beautiful and can make all the difference to aphid numbers. Similarly a hyssop hedge makes an attractive fragrant edging to vegetables or flowers, and will also deter cabbage butterflies. Tall (1m/3ft) slightly scruffy red-flowered buckwheat (*Fagopyrum esculentum*) is completely irresistible to hoverflies and sits well at the back of a border, perhaps accompanied by the equally effective attractive blue-flowering *Phacelia tanacetifolia*. The non-invasive *Convolvulus tricolor*, with its pretty petunia-like flowers, is another firm favourite with friendly insects. It is fairly standard advice to plant nasturtiums to lure blackfly and woolly aphids away from other plants into large colonies where their predators can gorge, however you need to get your nasturtiums going early, they are not at all helpful if they do not flower until after your broad beans have been devastated, or all your echinops buds have been ruined.

Umbellifers attract lacewings, so include fennel, dill or angelica in your borders, or plant sweet cicely and cow parsley in more shady areas. Parasitic wasps and hoverflies are also drawn to flowering heads of dill and fennel, and let some parsley plants go to seed. Golden rod attracts ladybirds, parasitic wasps and spiders, which consume masses of unwelcome insects. Prince's feather and other amaranths also prove magnetic for ladybirds, for shield bugs that gorge on mites, and even for parasitic wasps and slug-hungry shiny ground beetles. As an added bonus they look dramatic in a border or planted in a block in the vegetable garden.

Some of the most cheerful annuals are equally popular with friendly insects. The yellow and white flowers of poached egg plant (*Limnanthes douglasii)* buzz with insects all day long, so sow it under herbaceous plants, shrubs and soft fruit. Both baby blue eyes (*Nemophila menziesii*) and candytuft (*Iberis umbellata)* are hoverfly favourites.

Birds can be pests, but if you net fruit and cover seedlings they become welcome visitors and, maybe, residents. Robins adore caterpillars and grubs, especially cutworms, starlings help to control gypsy moth and wireworm populations, tits and finches devour bud-frequenting insects, woodpeckers search out cranefly larvae and

Above: A robin returning to its nest with food for its young.

ants, and thrushes adore snails. Blackberry bushes are wildlife sanctuaries, the centres of the bushes provide dry places for birds to nest or slug-eating hedgehogs to hibernate, their late flowers feed insects in early autumn when food is getting short, and the fruit then feeds birds until winter. Shrubs such as pyracantha are excellent for winter cover as well as berries, and late winter-flowering *Viburnum* x *bodnantense* 'Dawn' is useful for its flowers.

Toads, frogs and dragonflies are helpful predators, keeping insects and slugs at bay, and it is amazing how they appear from nowhere once you provide even a small pond. Surround it with plants such as *Alchemilla mollis* and hostas that give cool moist shade for ground beetles and slow worms, the other great slug predators.

Weeds

A wildlife garden is every bit as much a managed environment as any other style of garden, so you need to control invasive weeds to prevent them choking out your chosen plants. There is no point, for example, in planting a new hedge, meadow or borders, or creating a woodland edge, only to have the weeds springing up and preventing the new plants from flourishing. As with everything else it is a matter of finding the right balance. Weeds do have their uses, and add to the diversity of life in any garden. Some, such as willowherb (*Epilobium* spp.) and nettles, act as host plants for various creatures, while deep-rooted weeds, such as docks or creeping rooted couch grass, can improve the soil structure and provide opportunities for soil life to flourish – adding to the overall health of your patch. Other weeds, such as thistles and cow parsley (*Anthriscus sylvestris*), are very beautiful when they flower and also attract bees, hoverflies and butterflies.

It is a funny thing about weeds – if you call them wildflowers they become desirable, but as weeds they are pariahs. Farmers traditionally see field poppies and corn cockles (*Agrostemma githago*) as weeds, but we are very happy to have them scattered around the garden. Herb Robert (*Geranium robertianum*) and scarlet pimpernel (*Anagallis arvensis*), speedwell (*Veronica* spp.), clover (*Trifolium pratense*), ground ivy (*Glechoma hederaceae*) and plantains (*Plantago* spp.) are often classified as weeds, but they are all very desirable in a wildflower garden, and all attract a wide variety of insect life.

In a small garden, where space is at a premium and every plant you choose needs to provide the maximum benefit for wildlife, you will probably opt for a patch of wildflowers rather than weeds, and allow some grass to grow long to host insects and butterflies. If you have a vegetable patch, leave a few plants of fat hen (*Chenopodium album*) and sow thistle (*Sonchus olearaceus*) to attract leafminers and aphids and keep them off your vegetables, pull them up before they seed. Bindweed (*Convolvulus arvensis*) is very beautiful and attracts ladybirds and hoverflies. In a larger garden a patch of willowherb will encourage scores of moths and butterflies, including the caterpillars of the dramatic elephant hawkmoth; flowering cow parsley is a wonderful insect plant.

You do need to control weeds to prevent them from colonising areas where they are not wanted, but you never need to use herbicides. If you manage your soil well and build it up to be rich and fertile, using plenty of organic matter as soil improver and mulch, weeds should never get out of control. You will never get rid of them because they have evolved such efficient strategies for spreading, cultivation is the key: always dig your soil thoroughly and weed it well before planting anything; this is as true when planting trees as when sowing wildflowers.

The risk when digging is that you break up the roots of invasive perennial weeds, such as dock, bindweed or dandelions, and every minute piece of root will make

another plant. So dig carefully, using a fork, and be prepared to go over a weedy area several times to remove every trace of root. Rotovation is often the only approachable way of digging up a large patch. Unfortunately you are bound to chop up the roots of the perennial weeds, potentially spreading them far and wide. Only ever rotovate when the ground is dry or you risk spreading weeds further, and remove weeds by hand after rotovating.

Couch grass is one of the most difficult weeds to eradicate, with ground elder a close second, and you need to be determined to clear them or they will choke other plants. You can smother them out by laying black plastic over the ground and leaving it for a year, but this is not good for the soil as it deprives it of air and water and kills soil organisms. The best way to beat them is by careful digging and hand weeding.

All annual and some perennial weeds spread by seed, so the best way to stop them spreading is to remove them before they set seed. There is a potential conflict here between the needs of wildlife and the needs of the gardener, because seeds are important food for birds, but if your garden contains a good diversity of plants there should be enough food from the seedheads of plants that you do want to keep. The best way of keeping borders and your vegetable patch clear of weeds is to handweed and hoe several times during the growing season. Although perennials should be dug out, even deep-rooted weeds, such as docks, can be controlled by hoeing if you hit them at the right time – they depend on stores of food in their thick roots, and these reserves are lowest just before they flower, so if you hit them then they may not have the strength to regenerate.

Seasonal clearing, pruning and trimming

Many plants need to be cut back regularly, to encourage them to put out strong new growth, and a wildlife gardener needs to be very conscious of the right time to trim. Hedge maintenance is particularly important, as you should never trim a hedge when birds are nesting, and you should leave as much cover as possible over winter, along with berries and seedheads. Late summer is a good time to tidy most hedges, when fledglings have left, but a native hedge should not be cut back until late winter, when all the hips, haws and berries have been eaten.

Do not burn prunings, this is a waste of natural resources. Ideally you should shred them and add them to your compost or, if you have a substantial quantity, leave them to compost in a separate pile before using them as a mulch in a shrubby or woodland edge area. A pile of prunings makes an excellent winter home for small mammals, such as hedgehogs, and as dead wood breaks down it makes the ideal home for many insects and invertebrates.

SEASONAL TASKS

September
Mow late-flowering wildflower meadows and rake clippings to encourage the flowers to grow more strongly than the grasses.
Make a pile of woody prunings and stems to shelter overwintering creatures.
Sow wildflower mixtures.
Purchase spring flowering bulbs.
Plant wildflower plugs.
Sow seeds of annual flowers in beds and borders.
Sow new wildflower meadows on poor soil.

October
Feed the birds.
Plant spring flowering bulbs.
Mulch borders and vegetable plot to provide cover.
Dig a pond.

November
Feed the birds.
Rake leaves off grass for composting – leave flowerbeds for overwintering wildlife.
Cut back ivy after flowering.
Plant bare root trees and hedges.

December
Feed the birds.
Keep water ice free.

Opposite page: Cow parsley is a delight in early summer and much favoured by insects.

Right: early spring blossom and bulbs are vital for birds and early-rising insects.

If you examine a piece of rotting wood carefully you will see evidence of the fungi and other organisms that help break it down, and it will probably have hundreds of very small holes drilled into its surface. These are openings to the homes of tiny wasps and flies of all sorts, which in turn attract the spiders which recognise logs as an easy source of prey. The soft centres of old logs are also home to all sorts of beetle larvae, including stag beetles, and you may find toads and newts sheltering under rotting logs, as well as snails, slugs, woodlice and an assortment of grubs.

Tidying up is a subject that causes some dissent among gardeners – whether to clear away plant debris in autumn, or to leave it to rot in situ. When you are gardening with wildlife in mind it is best to leave as much debris on the ground as possible to provide ground cover and protection for all the scuttling insects and grubs that will overwinter there, which in turn provide food for birds. You should also leave spent stalks standing as far as possible, as some will be hiding insect or butterfly eggs or chrysalises and others are a source of food. Even when they drop to the ground naturally, leave them for the same reasons, plus the fact that they provide cover. Allow the seedheads of perennials and grasses to stand for valuable bird food, the bonus is that many look very striking in a winter garden.

Some gardeners just have to tidy up, they cannot bear to leave everything to settle into gentle decay. If you are in this category – and most gardeners are tempted to undertake at least a superficial tidying purely for the delight of working in the garden late in the year – you must compensate for the loss of some food supplies or homes for wildlife by creating others.

For example, when you clear away spent stalks and leaves, replace them with a good layer of organic mulch. This gives ground-dwelling creatures the cover they need and keeps bare earth protected over winter. Put all the material you have collected on to the compost heap rather than burning it, so that any hidden creatures can escape. Similarly when you are clearing weed from a pond, at any time of year, always leave it on the edge of the pond for a day before adding it to the compost heap. There are bound to be creatures hiding in it, and they need to be able to get back into the water.

Spent leaves become a major feature in autumn gardens. If you have a woodland habitat they can be left where they fall; however, it is not a good idea to leave them on grass as they will soon turn into a soggy mess. Similarly, if you have planted a wildflower meadow you need to keep fertility low and avoid any input of extra organic matter, so collect the leaves and pile them up then leave them to rot into rich leaf mould. This will take about a year, after which you can mix them into your garden compost or use them as mulch. The one thing you should never do is burn leaves, as they are a valuable source of organic nutrients and damp leaf litter provides a home for thousands of tiny creatures, including slugs and snails, woodlice, nematodes, beetle grubs and countless micro-organisms.

Managing a wildlife garden means being aware of sustainability and therefore using natural resources sensitively. The less you have to import to maintain your garden, the better. So make your own compost and leaf mould, and try to conserve water. Mulching is one way of retaining moisture in flowerbeds and around newly planted trees and shrubs. This has numerous advantages. It prevents unhelpful weeds from

colonising, keeps the soil moist and prevents it drying out in hot weather or getting waterlogged in wet weather. In addition it shades the soil and reduces heat stress on plants and soil organisms. On top of all that mulch provides cover for small living creatures and helps the soil temperature to stay reasonably constant.

The best time to lay a layer of mulch – compost, manure, half-rotted straw, bark or woodchips – is when the soil is fairly wet in late autumn, and again in late spring. Before laying a spring mulch fork in or rake off any winter mulch that has not been incorporated into the soil. This allows the ground to warm up as well as giving birds the chance to pick through the soil to catch early rising grubs and insects. Keep the mulch off perennials until the plants put out new growth.

In autumn rake off excess summer mulch to let birds get at the grubs, insects and their eggs. Leave a heavy clay soil without mulch over the winter or it may get even more waterlogged as it struggles to incorporate the extra material mulch. Avoid woodchips, cocoashells or sawdust if you have clay soil, as these break down more slowly than other organic soil improvers and the decomposing process uses up nitrogen that the soil needs.

Awareness of water is important in a wildlife garden. Rainwater is preferable to tapwater for watering plants, and you should always use rainwater to top up a pond as some aquatic creatures may be sensitive to treated tap water. So make room for at least one rainwater butt. Most people leave their butt covered to stop insects laying their eggs in the water; however, as a wildlife gardener wants to attract insects, the more uncovered standing water there is the better. As the water becomes stagnant it will turn green and grow algae and bacteria, and as these develop a team of water cleaners will move in, made up of the larvae of gnats, mosquitoes and midges. These filter the bacteria and algae out of the water and eat it, leaving the water clean. During the summer large swarms of the adult insects will congregate around the water in late afternoon and early evening, providing a fast-food restaurant for swallows and bats.

Winter management in a wildlife garden is more management of wildlife than of the garden. You need to make sure there are plenty of hiding places – decaying logs, upturned flowerpots and bird boxes as well as climbing plants and shrubby cover. Birdbaths must be kept frost free in winter – and topped up in summer. Birds need to bathe regularly to help them maintain the fluffiest plumage to keep them warm in winter. Bird feeders should always be kept topped up too, as even the best planted wildlife garden is fairly sure to have a lean period in mid or late winter when there is precious little food available in the wild.

Opposite page: Take care not to disturb hibernating hedgehogs when clearing your garden.

3 Borders and beds

It is hard to imagine any garden without flowering plants, and the wider the range of plants you grow, the wider the range of wildlife you will attract. Obviously, a larger garden can support a greater variety of wildlife than a small one; however, tiny measures can be just as valuable. You do not need to plant a miniature woodland edge, a wildflower meadow or even a hedge to make a difference. Whether your patch includes large herbaceous borders or no more than a few containers, a windowbox or hanging baskets, with a little thought you can grow varieties of plants that will be perfect for butterflies and moths, insects and birds. A few windowboxes acting as emergency cafés may be crucially important to creatures trying to navigate through an otherwise barren area. Never underestimate the value of every measure that you take to help wildlife, however insignificant it seems. When you add all these small gestures together they really do contribute much more than the sum of their individual parts to the overall picture.

Traditional cottage gardens were probably the best any gardener could offer wildlife, with their wide mix of cultivated and wildflowers, and aromatic and healing herbs, along with a good selection of vegetables. Most flowers were the traditional favourites rather than modern hybrids, so tended to be the single blooms that provide more nectar than highly developed forms. The mass of annual and perennial plants growing together provided a diversity guaranteed to attract the most wildlife visitors and, of course, traditional cottage gardeners used no chemicals. Incidentally, the fact that cottage gardens contained vegetables effectively explodes the myth that vegetable growing and gardening for wildlife are mutually exclusive. If you invite lots of insects into your garden, you also attract predatory insects, along with the birds that feed off them, and small mammals. This ensures pests never get out of control. Hundreds of creatures feed primarily on nectar, pollen or seeds, so careful planting will invite beautiful butterflies and moths, bees and many songbirds into your garden, along with all the smaller flying insects, such as lacewings and hoverflies, that no garden can do without.

More creatures will be attracted to fairly dense areas of cover than to isolated islands containing a few flowers, so fill your beds well and do not leave expanses of bare soil for any time – large areas of unplanted soil are about as attractive to most creatures as closely mown lawns. If you are planting in containers, try and place them near other plants, though if you are gardening on a balcony, roof or in a tiny urban garden this may not be practical. An alternative is to place containers close to a wall, which will offer protection and shelter, as well as maximum warmth.

FLOWERS FOR NECTAR

Spring
Alyssum (**alyssum**)
Aubretia deltoidea (**aubretia**)
Ceanothus 'Concha' (**ceanothus**)
Centranthus ruber (**valerian**)
Erica spp. (**heather**)
Erysimum cheiri (**wallflower**)
Genista lydia (**broom**)
Hebe spp. (**hebe**)
Hyacinthus orientalis (**hyacinth**)
Lunaria annua (**honesty**)
Muscari spp. (**grape hyacinth**)
Myosotis (**forget-me-not**)
Primula vulgaris (**primrose**)
Prunus spinosa (**blackthorn**)
Rubus fruticosus (**bramble**)
Syringa vulgaris (**lilac**)

Above: *Ceanothus* 'Concha'.

Opposite page: A scented herb garden surrounded by mixed borders and hedges ensures abundant insect activity.

The ideal café border will contain a mixture of flowering and fruiting shrubs, herbaceous perennials, biennials and annuals. It should be in a sunny part of your garden. Identify the warmest and sunniest places in spring and autumn, then plant perennials including wallflowers and sedum there to make sure that insects have food sources as soon as they arise in spring until late into the autumn. In midsummer the sun reaches further so you will have more choice as to position, and remember there are more creatures around in the summer, so you should provide many more plants for them to enjoy.

You want any border to be colourful and interesting for as long as possible throughout the year, with spring being an especially important time as nature kickstarts into action and the first waves of insects and early pollinators emerge, including the butterflies that hibernate over winter and creep out of hibernation to sunny spots to feed. Aim to provide a source of food for as much of the year as possible, starting with late winter flowering shrubs and bulbs in very early spring, and leaving plants in your beds to run to seed – the standing seedheads will attract birds in late autumn and well into winter.

Nearly every gardener I know gets a bit of an urge to do some garden tidying in autumn, if only for the joy of working outside as winter closes in, but please resist this urge as far as you can! There may be tiny larvae of all sorts of insects and moths and butterflies curled up in dead leaves or seedpods, chrysalides attached to a blade of grass or a stalk, and goodness knows how many creatures may be hiding in the litter of fallen leaves and stalks lying on the ground. By leaving the garden to end the year at its own pace you are protecting dozens of creatures, and your borders will also be much more interesting to look at in winter than if you meticulously cleared away the end of season debris – the sight of hoar frost on standing (or even flopping) stems topped with skeletal seedheads is unforgettable.

Choosing plants

As ever, native plants are particularly useful, especially to a range of insects, moths and butterflies whose caterpillars feed off a narrow range of species. For example, the caterpillars of orange tip butterflies will only feed on lady's smock, sweet rocket, or honesty, although adults are more catholic in their tastes, enjoying a very wide range of flowers. However, non-native herbaceous plants can often be equally valuable for nectar. Probably the best-known are buddleia, which has a magnetic attraction for butterflies, and tobacco plants which are especially popular with moths. You will be able to enjoy a huge range of insects buzzing and flitting around

a bed of Mediterranean herbs as well as native ones; bees are happy with pollen from virtually any source, many butterflies try almost anything – with a particular penchant for members of the daisy (and dahlia) family, with their closely packed heads of short tubular florets. Birds are also not particularly fussy about the origin of their autumn berries and seeds, although they have their favourites. Whatever you plant, choose single varieties of flowers rather than doubles or pompoms, as the singles contain more nectar.

I could never be without roses in my garden, and they are wonderful for attracting beetles – and, of course, aphids to feed hoverflies and ladybirds – as well as providing food for birds, mice and crawling insects in autumn. Shrub roses are also usually buzzing with bees collecting pollen, but if you want to plant specifically for butterflies it is sad to admit that even the most glorious sweet-smelling, prolific or perfectly formed rose has no value, as roses do not provide nectar. So if you are short of space and have to choose between a rose and something else, be kind and plant something that will be more appreciated by the greatest number of garden visitors.

Wildflowers are particularly valuable for so many species of wildlife, and it has become increasingly common practice to plant them in borders among other garden plants. Some – including scabious, knapweed, marjoram, common fleabane, cranesbill and bird's foot trefoil – are quite happy growing among cultivated varieties, but if you have the space I favour a separate wildflower border. This is simply because the soil conditions that wildflowers prefer tend to be rather different from their cultivated relatives. You can grow the two together, but it takes that much more effort to keep everything happy, and I believe in as little intervention as possible. However, if space is limited you will probably want to mix them up to include as many favourites as possible – it is largely a matter of taste, and energy.

Seasonal planting

To give the widest choice to wildlife, you want to plant to provide food, pollen and nectar from early in the year. This means you need to select plants that will flower in succession from early spring until late autumn. You should provide plenty of summer variety, and have a good array of seedheads and fruits for autumn and winter supplies. You also need to be sure to include some important host plants where insects and butterflies can lay their eggs and complete their life cycles.

If you have space, include winter flowering shrubs, such as viburnums, witchhazel, mahonia and daphnes, which are particularly valuable for birds and for the earliest rising insects. Useful early spring flowers include wallflowers and aubretia, favoured

Above: A single container of summer favourites can enhance a contrasting habitat.

by white and orange tip butterflies and early pollinators. Primroses and hyacinths attract all sorts of insects, and pollen-rich crocuses are good for bees and birds. Plant orange-yellow crocus and you will be very popular with all the local sparrows, as they contain the yellow pigment carotene which sparrows need to brighten up their plumage for the breeding season. Forget-me-nots and sweet Williams appeal to hordes of insects, including butterflies, as does broom *(Genista lydia)*, which is an attractive spring plant. Pansies and violas are cheerful nectar plants in late spring, along with grape hyacinths, forget-me-nots and the valuable red valerian, which flowers from spring until late summer. Butterflies adore honesty and its seeds are equally popular with finches – and children. Then come lady's smock and sweet rocket, plus a host of other nectar-rich border perennials.

As a rule of thumb, include plenty of members of the daisy family, masses of scented flowers and herbs for insects and butterflies, and some plants that produce strong seedheads for birds to feed on. A buddleia deserves a place in every wildlife garden, and do not forget the annuals such as candytuft, clarkia, poppies, poached egg plants, sunflowers and amaranths, which produce wonderful seedheads after their generous

FLOWERS FOR NECTAR

Summer continued
Malcolmia maritima
(**Virginia stocks**)
Malva moschata (**musk mallow**)
Mentha spp. (**mint**)
Nepeta spp. (**catmint**)
Nicotiana sylvestris (**tobacco plant**)
Oenothera spp. (**evening primrose**)
Origanum vulgare (**marjoram**)
Phaseolus coccineus (**runner bean**)
Phlox paniculata (**phlox**)
Rudbeckia fulgida
(**black eyed Susan**)
Silene dioica (**red campion**)
Stachys officinalis (**betony**)
Stachys sylvatica (**hedge woundwort**)
Tagetes patula (**French marigold**)
Thymus vulgaris (**thyme**)
Verbascum bombyciferum
(**mullein**)
Viola spp. (**viola**)

Autumn
Aster novi-belgii
(**Michaelmas daisy**)
Dahlia spp. (**dahlia**)
Lonicera periclymenum
(**honeysuckle**)
Saponaria officinalis (**soapwort**)
Solidago (**golden rod**)
Succisa pratensis
(**Devil's bit scabious**)
Sedum spectabile (**ice plant**)
Tropaeolum majus (**nasturtium**)
Verbena bonariensis (**verbena**)

flowers. For the end of the year, try to include Michaelmas daisies and sedum, to provide a last heavy crop of nectar, and golden rod for insects and seeds. Some of the ornamental grasses, such as *Miscanthus sinensis* or golden oats *(Stipa gigantea)*, produce superb seedheads that look stunning as well as providing food for birds.

Containers

If you are gardening in very limited space, you can make good use of containers. Starting with bulbs, or perhaps heather, you can provide good food and nectar sources from early in the year. Traditional sun-loving summer bedding plants such as lobelia and marigolds provide copious supplies of nectar. Many herbs are quite happy growing in pots, and some, including tansy and mint, should only be grown in containers to prevent them spreading too vigorously.

However, you do not have to stick to common container subjects, there is no reason to feel too restricted in your choice of plants just because you cannot plant in open ground. I have seen perennial flowers, vegetables, fruit trees and soft fruit bushes growing very happily in containers, and with a bit of thought you can provide a good range of insect and bird attracting plants. The main point to remember is to keep permanent plantings very well watered and fed. This is important because few containers are big enough to create the conditions for a proper living soil with all its associated life, so plants will not benefit from the same range of soil organisms.

Try and provide a good range of flowering plants in containers, just as you would in a larger garden, to encourage diversity. Combined with climbing plants, for food and cover, and a supply of water, a container wildlife garden can be just as much a wildlife haven as any other. You could even grow a tub of nettles if you wanted to be very kind to insects and butterflies. Nettles attract a specific kind of greenfly, and this provides food for early ladybird and hoverfly larvae, which will then move on to feast on insect pests elsewhere. Aphids tend to be plant specific, but their predators are not so fussy. Nettles are also the preferred food plant of the caterpillars of five brilliantly coloured butterflies – red admirals, peacocks, small tortoiseshells, orange tips and commas. You can chop the nettles back in June when their job is done as the adults feed on different plants.

Favourite garden plants

The teasel *(Dipsacus fullonum)* is rarely planted in any except wild gardens. This is because it can be invasive if it really likes your soil – ideally alkaline, poor free-draining soil in sun. However, it really is a treasure if you can contain it where you want it. Teasels are biennials and plants emerge in their first spring as low growing, slightly prickly serrated rosettes of leaves; however, by the second year they shoot up rapidly into erect plants between 1–2m/3–6½ft tall, with pairs of leaves evenly spaced all the way up the stem. Where these leaves join the stems they are hollowed, perfectly formed to catch little pools of water that provide drinks for many little birds and insects. In early summer the teasels blossom, beginning as soft green eggs that gradually colour up with row upon row of mauveish-pink flowers full of pollen, always covered with eager bumblebees and butterflies. If this were not enough, when flowering is over the heads turn deep brown, hard and bristly, and contain chambers full of seeds which are by far the most popular in the garden for goldfinches, that will descend in droves. The collective noun for goldfinches is a charm, and it is certainly one of the most charming early winter sights to see them fluttering around the heads of teasels, prising out the seeds.

My last garden was on a very sunny, warm dry hillside where teasels threatened to

Below: Teasel seeds are absolute favourites for goldfinches.

Above: Tall yellow mullein spires will be stripped by stripey mullein moth caterpillars.

Opposite page: Cheerful and easy to grow, poached egg plants are full of nectar.

become rampant. There were times when I cursed their vigorous spread, but the goldfinch bonus meant that the curses never lasted long. Teasels had always grown prolifically in that area, and were used to tease out the fine woollen cloth that the local valleys were famous for. In fact they are still used in some mills for just this purpose, as no-one has ever been able to come up with a manmade invention that does the job as well. In the garden you may need to keep them under check, pulling out each rosette of leaves with their long tap roots when they appear in spring, but they are statuesque and beautiful from spring until winter, so are worth the bother.

Members of the thistle family are almost as popular with insects and birds, and if you do not want thistles themselves, plant globe thistles *(Echinops ritro)*. As tall and erect as teasels, these attractive perennials produce round, prickly, blue or white blossoms on branching stems above spiny leaves. The flowerheads are very popular with all kinds of insects – including blackfly, so they make a useful decorative display around a vegetable garden to lure the flies off your broad beans until the aphid-eating insects do their work. Echinops means hedgehog in Greek, and the flowers turn into stiff, greyish-brown spiny seedheads that give the plants their name. The heads stand well into the winter, until they too are eaten by goldfinches and other seed-feeding birds. Another prolific seed-producing ornamental is the sunflower *(Helianthus annuus)*, which is another nectar-rich favourite with insects when it is flowering. It is also extremely popular with birds, which devour its seeds. Do include a few towards the back of your beds, or supported against a wall. You do not have to stick with the traditional bright yellow form, as there are a number of delicious dark reddish and bronze varieties that are just as attractive to wildlife.

The native mullein *(Verbascum bombyciferum)* is one of the easiest plants to grow, and looks stunning at the back of any border, with its huge spike of yellow and brown flowers in summer, above large greyish felty leaves. Biennial, it self seeds prolifically, which is usually a bonus; however, if you feel you have too many they are easily uprooted. The flowers attract bees and butterflies and the seedheads are a favourite home for ladybirds to overwinter, while the leaves are food for the spectacular stripy mullein moth caterpillar. These are venerable plants – in medieval times seedheads were dipped in wax and used as candles when rushes were not available. Most gardeners today seem to prefer the slightly more delicate modern varieties, with attractive coloured flowers in every pastel shade, some with strikingly different coloured centres, but although these plants seem equally attractive to wildlife, they can be disappointingly short lived.

Foxgloves are among my all-time favourite plants, worth growing just to watch the

bees plundering each intricately marked bell and emerging slumberous, laden down by pollen. Equally at home in a border or naturalising on a woodland edge, you must give them time to spread, as they are biennial and can be reluctant to germinate in the first few years. Once they like your garden, however, they spread so happily that you will probably be digging up boxes of seedlings to give to friends each year.

Nearer the ground, one of the most potent plants is the annual cherry pie *(Heliotropium)*. This little mound-forming plant was incredibly popular in cottage gardens for centuries, but has dropped out of fashion, perhaps because it is so tender that it must be the last plant out in spring. Its compact cushions of deep purple flowers are wonderfully fragrant and attract swarms of butterflies, hoverflies and bees. It is not just wildlife that find it appealing, it is one of those plants you can scarcely resist burying your face in, to drink in its incredibly powerful scent.

Other irresistible annuals in the wildlife garden are the yellow and white flowers of poached egg plant *(Limnanthes douglasii)*, which buzz with insects all day long, baby blue eyes *(Nemophila menziesii)* and candytuft *(Iberis umbellata)*, which are bee, hoverfly and butterfly favourites. Another joy of these annuals is that they are incredibly easy to raise, child's play in fact. So, if you have the space, give your children a patch of prepared earth, a packet of candytuft, baby blue eyes and perhaps cornflowers, marigolds and poppy seeds. The flowers are virtually guaranteed to flourish, giving the children a sea of bright flowers and their own little wildlife habitat.

The colours and shapes of flowers can matter when you are planting specifically to attract wildlife. The colours that most appeal to butterflies seem to be reds, blues, mauves and purples. They see a much wider range of colours than we do, right into the ultraviolet spectrum, and many flowers have nectar guides around the centre that are invisible to humans, except under ultraviolet light. These help butterflies to navigate, ensuring successful pollination for the flower. Moths may even be able to see infrared, picking up the heat emitted by plants on the darkest of nights. Hoverflies seem to be drawn mainly to oranges and yellows, while many small insects, such as thrips and fleabeetles, are pulled to yellow flowers, which then attract the insects that prey upon them. Birds feed first upon black, red and orange berries, while pink and white ones are the least attractive to them. You can use their colour preferences to your advantage, for example, as birds do not like red or copper, they will avoid red and bronze lettuces, and they won't touch red-leaved cabbages.

Butterflies are not particularly interested in the shape of a flower, their long tongues allow them to suck out nectar from even narrow, tubular flowers, and bees are very happy to crawl right inside any blossom. Some flowers, such as broad beans, will only open up for the heavy presence of a bumblebee. Lacewings, vital visitors to your garden in controlling aphids, prefer the flat heads of umbellifers, so always include fennel, dill or angelica in your beds, and let some parsley plants run to seed among your vegetables.

Butterfly beds

Scented flowers are vital in any wildlife garden. The scents of flowers often mimic the pheromones with which butterflies and moths attract mates, so the fragrance draws the insects to the plant, where they are rewarded by nectar and act as pollinators. Most highly scented flowers are winners, but vanilla seems to seduce butterflies above all other smells. Heliotropes and ivy flowers are firm favourites, as well as buddleia, which rightly deserves its title the butterfly bush. In summer buddleia bushes may be covered with butterflies, including peacocks, tortoiseshells, red admirals, brimstones, painted ladies and commas, whites, and even meadow browns and gatekeepers.

Below: Every wildlife garden should include a buddleia if there's space.

Right: Strongly scented tobacco plants lure moths and night-flying insects – which then attract bats.

White butterflies are attracted to plants containing mustard oils, including wallflowers, aubrietas and all members of the cabbage family, as well as mignonette and nasturtium. They are also fussy about colour, and only ever lay on green cabbages, leaving red (or variegated) cabbage leaves well alone. Their need for brassicas is a rather mixed blessing in the vegetable patch, as every gardener faced with a row of decimated cabbage plants knows all too well. However, if you plant a row of sacrificial cabbages, or some mustard or rape well away from the brassicas you want to protect, you should not have too much trouble with caterpillars. Otherwise you will need to be vigilant, picking them off by hand, or protecting the plants with fine netting to discourage the butterflies from alighting on them to lay their eggs.

Night-scented species, such as evening primrose and tobacco plants, attract a huge spectrum of moths. When choosing a tobacco plant avoid the emasculated scentless dwarf varieties too often sold as summer bedding and seek out *Nicotiana sylvestris*, the tall white form, which gives out an incomparable scent on summer evenings and glows like bright moonlight as the light fades. At dusk they expand their luminous starry flowers and invite moths in, even the big hawkmoths such as the migrant convolvulus hawkmoth, which is so large you may even mistake it for a small bat. Other scented favourites for moths and butterflies include sweet Williams, night-scented stock, sweet rocket and white jasmine. Honeysuckle is the food plant for the caterpillars of a great number of moths and a potent nectar source for many more, including hawkmoths, gold spangles and the silver-Y moth, as well as numerous butterflies. Honeysuckle is also a favourite bee plant, and will be buzzing with small insects on any sunny day. Plant the native form *Lonicera periclymenum*, as hybrids are fine as nectar plants, but not as food plants for caterpillars.

If your space is limited and you have to make a fairly narrow choice of butterfly plants, then the top ten nectar plants are buddleia, sedum, lavender, Michaelmas daisy, marjoram, aubretia, red valerian, French marigold, hebe and candytuft.

Herbs

All helpful insects, as well as bees and butterflies, like aromatic herbs, so a sunny herb garden is likely to be the busiest place in your garden in high summer. You can also plant borage, hyssop, sages and lavenders in your flower or vegetable beds, and grow different varieties of mints in pots. All attract helpful insects and bees and in fact mint is almost as attractive to butterflies as buddleia, and sparrows head for sage at nesting time. They line their nests with the aromatic leaves; I do not know why, but there is sure to be a reason for it. Rosemary is another favourite for bees, and lemon balm attracts dozens of insects. The graceful, pale blue flowers of chicory attract insects and butterflies in summer, followed by the birds which love the seeds. Chicory is another old country garden plant; it was once known as shepherd's clock as it is possible to estimate the time from it – its flowers close at noon.

A few lavender plants among your roses not only make delightful companions, they can also help prevent infestations of greenfly. A lavender or hyssop hedge makes an attractive fragrant edging to beds of vegetables or flowers, and one that will be particularly popular with hoverflies. Marjoram is another bee, butterfly and insect favourite. Chives look beautiful on their own and are also attractive as short hedges, edging paths or beds of other herbs. Bees adore them, and will buzz in and out of the flowers all day long in summer.

Above: Chives are particularly useful edging vegetable beds. They attract helpful insects and repel carrotflies.

4 Small and wild

Opposite page: Size is no barrier to creating a wildlife garden with a range of habitats for food and shelter.

There was a time when towns and cities were urban wastelands, highly polluted and fairly devoid of the wildlife which thrived in the countryside. That has all changed, and in many ways urban areas now offer more hospitable environments for a great deal of wildlife than much of the countryside.

There are limitations of course, towns and cities can never replicate all rural habitats, but where old industrial sites on the edges of cities, such as coalmines or iron workings, have been reclaimed as public amenity land, you can now find skylarks, hares and many other mammals, as well as a healthy spread of wildflowers. Urban foxes thrive, owls live happily on tall buildings, high-rise gardeners are reporting increased sightings of hawks swooping down and feeding on smaller birds that call in to roof gardens and balconies for food, and squirrels are common on roofs and in urban trees. Even otters are now being spotted in city centres, happy in the undergrowth and wasteland beside old canals and waterways yet within metres of busy roads and highly populated areas.

Creatures that are struggling to survive in the countryside often do well in urban habitats. Hedgehogs, declining in rural areas, are reported right in the middle of busy cities, frog numbers have plummeted in the countryside but increased overall thanks to urban garden ponds, and butterflies and moths are on the increase in towns while struggling in many of their traditional haunts.

One factor in this growth of wildlife is the decrease in urban pollution through better controls and awareness, compared with increased pollution from agricultural chemicals in the country. But much of the credit can go to enlightened gardeners for inviting in creatures whose natural habitats have been diminishing. Local authorities can also take some of the credit, and many public spaces now boast areas of wildflowers rather than the traditional fare of bare lawn and Keep Off The Grass signs.

Size is not crucial

The smallest gardens can be turned into pleasurable haunts for wildlife; it just depends on the scale of the wildlife as well as the scale of the garden. A few nectar-producing flowers in containers, a single fruiting tree, a short stretch of native hedge, a covering of ivy or a sink pond can all make a huge difference to the welfare of wildlife. A small tub of water will bring insects and their predators, and may attract frogs as well as birds. If you have a few flowering plants growing in a bit of soil a robin is likely to join you, along with many insects and perhaps some butterflies; a patch of low level planting

Above: A small pond provides opportunities for diverse and attractive planting.

or old leaves and rotting vegetation will host hundreds of insects and beetles and you are likely to see wrens scrabbling about, and maybe even a hedgehog. Even the tiniest of gardens can attract a host of insects, invertebrates, butterflies, squirrels, birds and hedgehogs, and urban foxes and even badgers may visit city gardens, even if there is not enough space for them to live there.

The best small wildlife gardens are full of plants: in beds, troughs or containers, or covering walls, which provide food and cover, and you must also have a source of water. Where you have got limited space, do not waste it on a lawn. If you really want a small patch of grass, plant it with wildflowers and native grasses to encourage butterflies and grasshoppers. If your garden is shady or damp it is better to avoid grass and give the space to other plants or a pond.

A path winding through a mass of plants of varying heights (growing in beds, containers, or a mixture of the two), ideally with a tree at some point, makes a small patch seem larger and is much more hospitable to wildlife than a more open area. There is nothing wrong with paving, as you can put containers on it, but leave some cracks between the paving stones or a few patches of gravel to provide opportunities for planting. A bit of uncovered ground will allow you to grow deeper-rooted plants and so attract ground-dwelling insects and beetles. Most wild creatures are fairly secretive by nature, and like to scurry among undergrowth or fly from bush to bush rather than risk being in the open.

If your garden is sunny, make the most of it with lots of flowers, cottage garden style, herbs and, if there is room, some flowering shrubs. Eke out the growing season with bulbs and autumn flowering plants, such as asters and ice plants, and if you have room for a tree, choose something that looks good in late autumn, winter or early spring when the rest of the garden is looking less dramatic. If you have sunny walls then you are spoilt for choice with flowering climbers – you could even plant a fan-trained fig, peach or apricot. Just remember many creatures, as well as plants, will appreciate a bit of shade.

Another vital ingredient in any garden is somewhere to sit, so rather than having a seat on its own turn it into an arbour by using it as a framework for scented climbers and surrounding it with fragrant herbs and your favourite flowers. Similarly, place a simple pergola over a sunny sitting area, cover it with mesh then train grapevines and flowering plants up over it. A useful tip if you plant climbing roses up the pillars of a pergola or arch is to twine them round as much as you can to encourage them to flower lower down.

A cool shady garden is more challenging, but may be very attractive to lots of wild creatures. Even the most inauspicious of sites can contain climbers and a pond. If sunlight is very limited grow a few sun-loving plants in pots to provide nectar and attract some insects and their predators, then move the pots around to make the most of what sun there is. There are also plenty of perennials and grasses, as well as shrubs, that will thrive in light shade and provide a long season of interest.

If you have the space, you could turn the situation to your advantage by planting a tree or two, so creating a shady mini-woodland habitat. Underplant the trees with shrubs, bulbs and wildflowers – ground cover plants such as the evergreen periwinkle are very good value in a shady garden, and provide perfect shelter for ground beetles and amphibians. Some ornamental grasses, such as various members of the Pennisetum and Ophiopogon family, also perform well in shade, and although they are not native they will provide shelter for ground-dwelling creatures, while their seedheads will be popular with the birds.

Bamboo is another plant which provides excellent cover – as well as a good supply of garden sticks – and holly and box will both grow happily in partial shade. The bright yellow flowered *Mahonia japonica* is good for winter interest, while providing shelter and nectar, and ivy is, of course, the ideal climber for a shady place. Choose a silver

variegated form, such as *Hedera helix* 'Goldheart', which will shine out from a dark corner. Alternatively, grow the climbing hydrangea *(Hydrangea petiolaris)* and enjoy the fine sight of its creamy white flowers in early summer, followed by attractive autumn foliage.

All small gardens can boost their habitats with bird feeders and nesting boxes (see chapter nine), and you can encourage hedgehogs to hibernate in yours by piling up some logs or placing a special box in its most undisturbed part. If you want ground-dwelling creatures, leave some vegetation on part of the garden floor. Toads and newts will creep under upturned clay flowerpots or under stones, and lots of creatures will seek out the warmth of a compost heap. Even if your garden is not large enough to hold the diversity that may be necessary for creatures to stop and breed there, all gardens can offer food, water and some shelter.

The only proviso for a successful town wildlife garden is that there are other gardens nearby which can also act as staging points. Wildlife gardening is all about gardeners co-operating with nature, and in towns it also requires the co-operation of other gardeners to ensure there are enough places where creatures can rest, drink or feed, or even hide, as well as use as thoroughfares to the next port of call. If you are gardening in total isolation, with no complementary habitats in your area, you are sure to attract some winged creatures at the very least, but your best efforts will be less well rewarded than if yours is one among a network of green spaces, however tiny.

Fortunately, more and more urban gardeners are rising to the challenge of accommodating wildlife, and in many ways urban gardens (however tiny) have even more important roles to play than larger gardens outside town. I live in one of the few remaining genuinely rural areas of Britain, where farms are too small for intensive agriculture and there is little arable land. This means that the landscape has changed little and hedges still flourish as the most efficient method of stock protection. Our garden is large enough to include trees, shrubs and ground cover. We have native hedges and dry stone walls, fruiting trees and beds of flowers and vegetables. In addition there are wildflowers in the grass, under hedges and in the meadow; and there is water and wilderness, tangled undergrowth, as well as slightly tidier spaces. The garden replicates all sorts of local habitats and is chockful of flying, scuttling and creeping creatures; however, if something extraordinary happened and this garden no longer existed it would make precious little impact on the local wildlife population. However in the urban environment every container full of blossoms makes a significant difference. A hanging basket on the sunny balcony of a high-rise flat could mean the difference between life and death for a butterfly.

Opposite page: Containers and climbers help provide shelter and food in this tiny but beautiful garden.

First steps

The classic advice for anyone wanting to encourage wildlife is to buy a freestanding pond or simply dig a hole, line it and fill it with water. Next plant a few flowering perennials nearby and then sit back and wait for the creatures to arrive. As with the rest of life, water really is the key, and even a birdbath in an otherwise fairly barren environment will attract numerous aquatic insects, then the other insects and birds that prey upon them – within hours. If there are other ponds or watercourses nearby, frogs may follow within days. If not, import some spawn in spring, preferably taking it from a friend's pond rather than from the wild. In addition, a few nectar-rich flowers in a nearby sunny spot will attract butterflies; add a berried shrub, a tree in a container, or a covering of ivy on a wall, and birds will come to drink, bathe and may even stay to breed. If there is shelter on a nearby wall, bats may arrive to eat the insects and stay to roost.

The best place to put a small freestanding pond is in a sunny part of your garden so you have more choice of what you can plant around it, also butterflies and frogs are attracted to sunnier spaces. If you are making a mini pond from an old sink or even a bucket, try and start it off with a handful of mud or slime from an existing pond, as this will contain lots of microscopic and tiny pondlife and possibly bits of vegetation to give you a headstart. However tiny, include some plants to oxygenate the water – water milfoil or water starwort are free-floating and not too large. Also, surround the pond with plants (a group of containers close together is fine), as a pond in the middle of open space is less inviting than somewhere with cover or food close by.

If you are using a steep sided sink, float a disc of wood on the surface which insects can land on and use as a platform from which to drink; also place a few rocks inside one edge or drape a piece of furled chicken mesh over the side so that anything that falls in has a chance of scrambling out. You are often advised to leave a piece of wood resting on one of the edges of a steep pond as an escape plank, but in my experience this does not work very well as small mammals that fall into ponds tend to ignore it and scrabble round the edges looking for a foothold to help them climb out. A shelf of stones is the simplest precaution.

Trees and hedges

There is nothing like a tree to give a feeling of space and grace to a garden. Surprisingly, planting a tree often makes a small space feel bigger, as well as providing shape, stature and colour, along with, possibly, flowers and fruit. A tree sets the tone for a garden throughout the year, both when it is in full leaf and as an attractive skeleton in winter.

Opposite page: A silver birch demands little space and looks striking against any background.

Above: Climbers, flowers, shrubs and hedging plants transform an urban balcony or roof garden.

It also provides shelter and some shade and gives you the opportunity to grow plants underneath that would not be happy in borders or containers.

Planting a tree is probably the second most important step you can take to attract and support wildlife. A carefully chosen tree will bring birds and perhaps squirrels, as well as hordes of insects. Wildflowers and bulbs will thrive on the ground beneath it, and when the leaves drop in autumn they will provide cover for beetles, insects and grubs, and perhaps even a hedgehog.

In small gardens it is sensible to choose smaller trees, as a large specimen may throw too much shade which could restrict other planting. Large trees have widespread roots which may be a problem in a very built up area, and could cause difficulties with neighbours. One of the best native trees for a town garden is silver birch, with its very attractive shiny silvery-white stem in winter, and delicate foliage that casts a light shade. It does not need much space, so you can plant a small grove of three about 45cm/18in apart in the corner of a garden and encourage a mini woodland habitat beneath.

The rowan and crab apple are perfect for even quite tiny gardens, and holly is a magnificent tree that responds well to clipping, so can be kept at whatever size your garden dictates. Hazel is good value, with its spring catkins and autumn nuts, which will be a magnet for squirrels, and in a damp garden willow is an obvious choice for its pale green dancing foliage and bright yellow spring catkins, favourites with butterflies and early pollinators looking for food.

Willow is thirsty though, and should only be planted if you have a genuinely damp garden, otherwise it will leach water from its surroundings and deprive other plants of moisture. If a conifer appeals, consider a juniper, which has striking feathery foliage and a pleasant mid-green colour. Do think of natives first, as they enhance the wildlife value so much more than others. But choose carefully, as some natives are less wildlife friendly than others. The London plane, for instance, is a fine city tree that flourishes despite poor soil and pollution, but it supports very little life and is uninteresting to insects and consequently to the birds who rely on insects for their food.

When choosing a tree, you should also take notice of what is growing in the area. If there is a mature tree on your boundary, take advantage of all it offers and plant something different but complementary – for instance, if the tree next door is not a fruiting variety then choose something which provides blossom and fruits. Similarly, you may like to plant something evergreen if your neighbour's tree loses its leaves in winter; or if the tree next door has a very rounded head you could choose something with a different silhouette, such as a slim birch. Town gardening is about making the most of what is already there, as well as adding to it to create as diverse and sustainable habitats as possible.

Hedges in towns make excellent wildlife corridors, and if you have the space a hedge makes an ideal boundary. It can include fruiting and berrying shrubs, as well as those with beautiful stem and leaf colour, or you can plant a native thorn hedge to keep intruders out while providing a wonderful habitat. For a tall evergreen hedge, holly is the perfect urban choice, for something non-native choose privet or box before other species, and do not trim them back until after they have flowered. Green hedges seem to look best in an urban setting, while beech, which holds its brown winter leaves, tends to look rather dead. There is little more derelict-looking than a winter beech hedge adorned with bits of rubbish blown off the street.

Soil-less gardens

Whatever size your garden, even if it is only a balcony or a tiny roof terrace, with a bit of planning you can have something flowering all year round to attract the widest spread of insects and their predators. If you have no soil – which is very possible if you only have a small patio garden, a flat roof or balcony – you could build a raised bed or use containers to create a wonderful diversity of planting.

The choice of containers is huge, ranging from tiny pots, perfect for herbs, to large tubs suitable for small trees, so you can have a good variety for effect in your garden. There are containers to suit every taste and budget, from recycled sinks and old dustbins to ornate antique stone and metal pots. Galvanised buckets are popular, but should not be used for ericaceous or acid composts; metal containers also heat up and cool down quickly so you must watch the watering. Clay or terracotta pots usually remain gardeners' first choices, they are not expensive and they provide a better ratio of weight to soil than heavy stone containers, while providing similarly good thermal qualities, ensuring that compost stays warm for a long time and cools slowly. They are also sturdy enough to use for quite tall plantings, but light enough to move without too much trouble. Unglazed clay pots are porous, so water leaches out of them and you will need to water plants more often than those in glazed pots, but you can also use this to your advantage in a very sunny garden – if you fill large unglazed pots with water and place them where they catch a breeze, water will evaporate on the outside of the pot to cool the air and the plants around.

Containers are a necessity in small spaces, but they are also a useful way of expanding the range of habitats in any garden as they allow you to create particular soil conditions. For example, you could grow acid-loving plants such as heathers or a camellia in an area of alkaline soil, or drought-loving candidates in a damp garden. You can also use containers to contain invasive plants, such as mints, tansy and nettles that are great for wildlife but rarely appreciated running wild. Another bonus is that you can move containers around, making the most of the sun, or use them as decoys: tubs of nasturtiums placed beside broad bean plants, for example, lure the aphids away from the vegetables, while a container of strong smelling chives or lavenders put next to carrots will confuse carrot flies, as these hunt by scent.

The disadvantage of containers is that their plants require more maintenance than those in the soil. This is partly because you have to keep a close eye on watering as the soil in pots can dry out very fast, but mainly because even a large container, such as a barrel, is too small to allow a living soil to build up. This means a container gardener will have to feed the soil regularly to make sure there are enough nutrients for plants to flourish. Only use good garden soil for large containers and permanent plantings (trees, for example), otherwise it is best to use potting compost, or half soil and half compost. Where weight has to be considered – on roofs and balconies, or when you are planting extremely heavy pots that you may want to move at some point – always use lightweight compost with water-retaining granules.

You can grow just about anything in a container. I have seen forest trees growing in tubs, so if you really want an oak tree on a patio, or even a balcony, you can have one, as long as you keep its roots and branches well pruned and keep it out of full sun. Small native trees, such as rowan or crab apple, are quite happy with their roots contained, and orchard fruit trees will flourish, provided you choose varieties grafted

on to dwarfing rootstock. If you want a fruit tree in a tiny garden, it is always best to choose a traditional variety rather than opting for a modern hybrid marketed specially for growing in tubs on patios. These modern varieties tend to be rather unnatural shapes and, although they are designed to fruit heavily without putting on much growth, they tend to look sickly quite quickly without a good deal of care; they also seem unable to flourish in an organic regime.

The other method of growing plants in a soil-less garden is in raised beds. These are quite simple to construct and create a wonderful illusion of space in a small garden. They are also very easy to maintain, as you do not have to bend over. First you need to build some sturdy sides. Wooden panels are easy but you could build a dry stone wall, which will contain the soil while providing a useful habitat in itself – its cracks and crevices make perfect hiding places for insects, spiders and even small amphibians and mammals. If you are making the bed on a hard surface, such as concrete, you should break up this surface as much as possible, then put in a layer of hardcore or small stones about 30cm/1ft deep before adding the growing medium. The medium you choose will depend on what you want to grow; for example, if you want a bed of Mediterranean herbs which will be delightful when you brush past and great insect attractants, you will need good drainage, so incorporate plenty of grit with your topsoil and compost. For a mini-wildflower patch, avoid adding any organic matter to your soil as the fertility must be kept in check. Deep-rooting plants require more fertile soil, so mix a good dose of manure or compost in with the topsoil. Plants look wonderful tumbling over the edge of a raised bed, and if you build the sides out of stone flowers such as tall valerian and low-growing aubretia will be content growing in the wall.

The classic soil-less garden is on a roof. The first thing to do if you are planning a roof garden is to make sure the roof will take the weight – you may need to ask a surveyor to check it – and remember that you will need easy access to water. With any roof garden, shelter is a priority. This is not just for privacy but because conditions are always more extreme than at ground level, hotter in summer, cooler in winter, and windier year round. The biggest challenge is always the wind and the higher the space, the greater the chance of wind damage. So when deciding upon planting start by thinking about how you can deflect the wind and shelter anything you plant.

One of the most effective wind barriers is a native hedge, which will grow quite happily high up. A mixture of thorns, crab apple, hazel and guelder rose works well – use three-year-old container-grown plants rather than young bare-rooted specimens, and plant them on the side of the prevailing wind, in a trough to spread the weight around the edge of the roof. You will attract masses of insects and birds to the flowers, berries and fruit, and you may even get squirrels for the hazelnuts if there are tall trees nearby.

Once you have sorted out a wind barrier, you can plant most things on a roof garden, and you are sure to attract all sorts of flying creatures, although you will not have ground level wildlife as it is impossible to create the humus-rich floor or dense ground cover planting that they like.

Whether or not you plant a native tree or hedge, you should always try to include flowering bulbs, perennials and annuals for insects, bees and butterflies. Herbs are particularly useful insect attractants and some, including lovage and chervil, will grow in rather damp shady corners. Choose lightweight containers, and place different sized pots closely together to create a pleasing grouping of different heights; this will also provide cover and areas where creatures can hide. Include some erect stemmed plants and some with droopy foliage. There is no reason not to include vegetables in a tiny garden, many will grow quite happily and decoratively in containers and attract all sorts of insects and their predators, and you may even get something to eat. Tomatoes are an obvious choice for a sunny summer garden, salad leaves are easy, coloured chard is very decorative, and a green-leaved cabbage or two will bring in white butterflies.

If you live in a flat you may have nowhere but a windowbox to garden, but you can still have insects, butterflies and birds visiting, though you will not be able to offer

Opposite page: Tiered beds maximise the space and allow a wide range of plants to grow on this city roof.

them space to reside. Try and keep your windowbox filled with flowering plants from early to late in the year. Primroses and yellow crocus are bright early on and attract many insects (as well as sparrows and tits, which may like them too much and peck them to bits), perhaps followed by wildflowers, as these tend to thrive in containers because they do not mind a bit of neglect. Annual poppies and cornflowers provide a bright summer display, and perennials, including cowslips, knapweed and harebells put on a good show.

If you plant border flowers, go for single varieties, which produce the most nectar. A wonderful choice for any container and perfect for a windowbox, the tobacco plant *(Nicotiana sylvestris)* lures dozens of moths on warm summer evenings, looks luminous outside a window and spreads a wonderful scent. Fragrant herbs are also very good candidates for windowboxes, bringing lots of insect life along with their delicious scents – and you can use them in the kitchen. Or you could grow a climber, such as scented jasmine, on a framework around a window, although you will only be able to keep it under control if your windowbox is on the ground floor.

Hanging baskets and wall-mounted containers are particularly useful on balconies – you do not need to stick to the traditional summer bedding plants to have a good display, try spring bulbs surrounded with evergreen foliage or low-growing summer-flowering wildflowers. The problem with hanging baskets is that they dry out quickly so they are no good for plants that like damp conditions, but otherwise they are pretty adaptable.

Baskets should always be well lined with coir matting or moss gathered from your garden or bought, not taken from the countryside. As raised baskets are seen from underneath, trailing plants are important. Periwinkle *(Vinca minor)* can be used in a year-round basket, attracting insects and butterflies, and ivy is an obvious choice. Nasturtiums are prime candidates for summer baskets, attracting visitors well into the autumn. Alpine strawberries *(Fragaria vesca)* look wonderful in baskets, providing flowers, interesting foliage and masses of fruit – sure to attract birds if the humans do not get there first.

Green walls

The plants that make the most difference of all in a tiny space are the climbers. If your walls are well clothed you will attract numerous insects and birds to breed as well as feed. Nearly every garden offers scope for some living walls of climbing plants, and there are climbers for cold and shaded walls as well as sunnier aspects. If you do not have suitable walls for climbers, improvise. You can erect trellis or stretch wires above

Opposite page: A well-trained fruit tree underplanted with herbs and foliage plants for food and cover.

a low wall or fence and grow climbers along the framework. If you are on a tight budget, one of the most effective methods of creating a living boundary is to install a mesh fence and attach arches made of willow or hazel to the upright posts, then string wire between them. I did this against a boundary in a former garden, and within two years the mesh was completely hidden and climbers had ascended the arches and were taking over the space between them; a year later the whole structure was clothed. Willow and hazel do not last for ever, but if you make the arches out of a double row of withies it has a better chance of lasting longer, and when one rots it is easy to slip it out and insert another.

Climbers are very useful on high-rise gardens, whether roofs or balconies. For a balcony it is wise to place a trough at one end to spread the weight, rather than a single pot, and train climbing plants over the edge of the balcony, twining it around supports if there are any, or fastening it carefully to the balcony wall with suitable nails and twine. Climbers can be used instead of a hedge to filter wind on a roof garden, but it may take a while for them to get established precisely because of that chill wind factor. Honeysuckle is one of the most resilient climbers, and once it is established you can plant others alongside it which will benefit from the slight shelter it will afford. Climbing roses will not thank you for being planted as a wind screen, nor will passion flowers, but you can plant them happily on a roof garden once some shelter is in place.

Many climbers can be grown in containers – the larger the better, a half barrel is ideal – or in the ground. If you are planting in the ground always place them at least 30cm/1ft away from the wall to avoid the dry rain shadow area. This will also make them less likely to try and grow into any foundations. The one caveat about climbers in small town gardens concerns the worst urban predator, the cat. You need to aim for thick bushy cover so that cats cannot get easy access to hunt and raid birds' nests. Thorny shrubs, such as berberis, placed at the bottom of a wall provide excellent protection, although an alternative is to leave the lower stem of a climber fairly bare and encourage it to branch and bush out from around 2m/6½ft above the ground; also, only plant low-growing plants at its base. These precautions will ensure cats do not have an easy climb and give them nowhere to hide at ground level.

Ivy is the number one choice as a climber. It offers such a versatile habitat – cover and shelter, nesting opportunities, leafy food for the holly blue caterpillar, flowers and fruit for birds, and nectar right into autumn for insects and butterflies on sunny days. It is evergreen, there are varieties with shining silver or gold edges to shimmer from dark corners, it grows fast and requires no maintenance apart from trimming if it gets out of hand and before it twines round gutters and into eaves. You do not even have to support it.

Above: Violas, petunias and marigolds in a windowbox invite insects and butterflies.

Second best for a chilly north or east-facing wall is the climbing hydrangea *(Hydrangea petiolaris)*. This is also self-supporting and provides quantities of nectar for butterflies, as well as shelter for birds and bats. Honeysuckle will also grow on a cool wall. It offers cover, nectar for moths and butterflies and berries for birds, and, of course, throws its wonderful scent around a small garden. You will need to provide a sturdy framework for honeysuckle, its thick twining stems support a mass of branches and foliage and it becomes very heavy with age. The easiest frameworks are simply wires stretched between vine eyes, specially designed fixings that keep the wires about 10cm/4in away from the wall, allowing a small corridor behind the plants where creatures can shelter.

Climbing roses are among the most beautiful plants if you have the space; their rewards are so great, with glorious scented blossoms all summer long followed by bright hips. Happiest on an east or west-facing wall, roses do not have a universally good press. They are surrounded by unhelpful myths about their temperamental and demanding nature, about the need to spray and pinch and trim and chop and prune and feed, but these tales are largely nonsense. If you choose old varieties of roses, plant

them in a generous planting hole backfilled with copious amounts of muck and keep them well watered as they are establishing themselves, they will look after themselves thereafter. Yes they do attract greenfly, but this is an advantage in a wildlife garden, aphids feed hoverflies, lacewings and ladybirds, as well as birds. Moreover they attract scores of beetles, their autumn hips are food for birds, insects and even mice, and their tangled stems are a favourite place for blackbirds to nest. In a small garden they are particularly good value as a covering for walls and arches or other free-standing structures. The only disadvantage of roses is they are not butterfly plants, so if it is butterflies you want to attract you are better off with honeysuckle.

Other valuable wildlife climbers include wisteria. This is perfect for a south-facing wall, its heavy blossoms are nectar rich and its strong woody stems provide good nest-building opportunities for summer nesting birds. Native hops (*Humulus lupus*) will cover an east-facing wall in no time, attracting loads of insects and providing food for the caterpillar of the comma butterfly. A pillow filled with dried hop flowers is a traditional soothing remedy for sleeplessness. Grapevines on a sunny wall provide fruit for moths, butterflies and birds, and you can train pyracantha against a wall to provide excellent cover for birds, with its copious berries and nectar ensuring a plentiful supply of food. Many species of clematis are good for bird cover and nectar, and their fluffy seedheads also provide food. Any vigorous variety will attract the birds; however, if you have the space allow the native traveller's joy (*Clematis vitalba*) to romp over a cool wall.

Most climbers are valuable, and will at the very least provide nectar and food for insects and attract birds into your garden. The gloriously prolific and long-flowering passion flower *(Passiflora incana)* is a personal favourite, perhaps growing above ornamental quince *(Chaenomeles japonica)*, which makes a very attractive wall shrub and provides early nectar in spring. Leave a patch of sunny, south-facing wall bare among the profusion of greenery and blossoms, to allow hunting spiders to seek their prey and butterflies to bask in the warmth.

Stones and logs

Most rockery and alpine plants are very small, which means you can get a huge variety into a small space to attract butterflies, moths and other flying insects, while providing the ideal habitat for many more creatures. Spiders live in dry holes in walls, toads and newts may overwinter there, beetles, earwigs, slugs and snails love them, and the soil-dwelling creatures will feed birds and carnivorous insects.

Dry stone walls around raised beds are perhaps the easiest way of introducing the

Opposite page: Honeysuckle is one of the richest nectar plants and offers excellent cover.

Above: Containers can be used for permanent plantings where there's no access to soil.

rockery type habitat into a garden, as you can leave gaps between the stones and snuggle plants into the crevices. A rockery feature need be no more than a pile of selected stones on top of a heap of soil. Garden centres sell mountains of limestone specially excavated for rockeries, but please do not buy it, as the extraction of water-worn limestone has caused the destruction of some of the country's most fragile habitats. It is always best to use local stone wherever possible, it may be the most appropriate for mosses and lichens to colonise and will be familiar to creatures moving through your area, or staying. It is also often free, particularly when someone has repaired a wall or excavated a patch of garden.

In fact it is best to use local materials for everything in a garden wherever possible, from seating to landscaping, planting to paving. This is not just a question of aesthetics, although if there is a strong local architecture or building style local materials will fit into any scheme better than those from outside the area. The argument is more along the lines of that put forward for planting natives, local wildlife may be more at home in familiar materials, and may even have evolved a relationship with them. Also, wildlife gardening should be sustainable, and it is always more sustainable to use locally produced goods than those imported from afar.

Many creatures will thank you if you leave a small log pile in a quiet corner, preferably with some slightly rotting logs among them. Hedgehogs will crawl into the dry middle to hibernate, woodboring insects and beetle grubs will make their homes in the soft centre of any rotting logs, and spiders will roam around hunting. If you have to remove a tree from your garden leave the stump if possible. Tree stumps are great for insects and you will get some interesting mosses and fungi developing as they decay.

The only time a stump or decaying logs have to be removed is when honey fungus was to blame for the tree's demise. If this was so, it is vital to dig out the entire root and surrounding area, clear any dead wood and twigs from around the tree and burn them, then disinfect the ground with armillatox or another proprietary fungicide. This is probably the only occasion when I would recommend using any chemical in your garden, as unfortunately when honey fungus appears it spreads like wildfire, quickly infecting any trees its long threads reach under the ground. You may spot early signs as branches die back, or white spots of fungus appear on dying wood, but often the first real indication is the appearance of clumps of yellow fungus around the base in autumn – but by then the damage is done.

As ever, sickly trees are most at risk, so try and keep your trees healthy by practising good garden management. Never leave decaying wood from suspect trees lying around in wood piles and keep it away from the compost heap. Make sure trees are kept well watered and that they do not suffer insect damage, also remove damaged branches and keep your trees well pruned. You must also keep an eye on leaf colour, if leaves start to yellow, turn crinkly brown around the edges, or the veins begin to stand out, the tree is probably not getting the minerals it requires and you will need to feed the soil.

5 Hedges, thickets and vertical cover

Opposite page: Blossoming blackthorn hedges are a welcome indicator of spring, and an important home to hundreds of insects, butterflies, birds and small mammals.

Every garden, whatever its size and situation, has boundaries, and how you treat these, which materials you choose for them, can really make a difference to wildlife. You may have inherited fences, which on their own are pretty sterile environments, yet add climbers and shrubby cover and you provide shelter and food, making them very useful habitats. You can also cover walls with climbers, a particularly helpful move where tall buildings form boundaries, while traditional stone or old brick walls may already be useful habitats as they are often filled with hollows, nooks and crannies that are very attractive to lots of insects and invertebrates, plus the occasional small mammal. Expanses of sunny wall prove irresistible to basking butterflies and hunting spiders. However, if you have the choice, the best boundary to attract and protect a whole array of wildlife is always a hedge. Hedges can also form vital links between green areas, linking gardens with other gardens and parkland, or with old areas of woodland.

Attractive and versatile, a hedge enhances any landscape, as well as providing shelter and diffusing wind much more effectively than a fence or wall. So a hedge should always be the first choice for a windswept garden. A thick hedge ensures privacy, and if you plant thorny species it will keep intruders out. Besides their value as versatile wildlife habitats, hedges make a highly attractive backdrop to any garden, and an excellent foil for many flowering plants.

A hedge does take some degree of maintenance, and tall evergreen hedges or those with prickly leaves can appear very daunting, particularly for elderly gardeners, but you can let a native hedge run slightly wild, or decide on fairly low hedges that are easier to manage. The humble and unfashionable privet, for example, makes a good low, long-lasting, dense hedge. It is an excellent food source for any flying creatures, as it produces small white fragrant flowers, followed by tiny black berries. Privet hosts numerous insects, is an important source of food for butterflies and birds, and provides cover for lots of invertebrates and small mammals.

Preserving hedges

Hedgerows are a manmade habitat, but one of the most valuable in the garden, and they have been a particular feature of many regions of the landscape for thousands of years. They were first planted, perhaps as far back as the Bronze Age, because farmers needed them to separate and shelter livestock, and to demarcate clearings and fields

from what was once largely woodland and scrub. For millennia they divided the countryside into a patchwork of small fields, and the cover, shelter, food and conditions provided by these native country hedges proved an excellent habitat for a vast array of rare and common wildflowers, as well as for birds, insects and mammals. Almost 1,000 native plant species have been recorded in Britain's hedges and verges, along with the varied wildlife associated with them.

Sadly, from the late 1940s on, intensive modern agriculture enabled many farmers to replace pastures with crops, and large agricultural machinery made small fields impractical. Even on farms that retained livestock, barbed wire seemed cheaper than keeping up a hedge. Until the late 1980s, the British government actually paid farmers a subsidy to tear out their hedges.

As hedges went, so did much wildlife. Farmland birds have decreased in number and range, among them song thrushes, linnets, bullfinches and corn buntings. Most of our resident birds breed or feed in hedgerows, such as the hedge sparrow, wren and goldfinch, song thrush, yellowhammer, whitethroat and bullfinch. Migrants also need our hedges – including whitethroats and blackcaps, here from Africa for the summer, and redwings escaping the Scandinavian winter. Bats roost in tree hollows by day and cruise the hedgerows for food at night, and hedgehogs, voles, shrews and mice, as well as the rare dormouse use hedges for shelter and food. Country hedges may also offer shelter to stoats and weasels as well as rabbits and badgers, and invertebrates are common in most hedges but especially thrive on old and overgrown ones.

Butterflies breed and feed in hedgerows, with over a hundred types of moth feeding on hawthorn alone, and nearly as many on blackthorn. A hedge full of blossom and catkins in spring will provide food for butterflies emerging out of hibernation. Unfortunately, methods used to maintain hedges can reduce their value to wildlife, particularly breeding butterflies. Many moths and butterflies lay their eggs in autumn on specific hedge species; however, farmers generally use a flail to trim hedges in late autumn and the flail takes out most of the new growth, including the butterfly eggs.

Opposite page: Wrens hunt for food in the undergrowth beneath a hedge.

Below: Evergreen privet supports many butterflies as well as birds.

HEDGING PLANTS

Acer campestre (**field maple**) Fast-growing native plant, suitable for growing as a hedge or tree. Rich, golden autumn colour. Lime tolerant. Plant 45cm/18in apart for hedges 120cm/4ft upwards.

Alnus cordata (**Italian alder**) Fast-growing native tree, producing catkins in spring. Bright green, glossy leaves. Suitable for wet and chalky positions. Plant 60cm/2ft apart for hedges 180cm/6ft upwards.

Alnus glutinosa (**common alder**) Fast-growing native tree with yellow catkins in early spring. Thrives in wet conditions. Plant 60cm/2ft apart for hedges 180cm/6ft upwards.

Berberis darwinii (**barbery**) Evergreen hedging plant with prickly, glossy, dark green leaves and beautiful dark orange flowers in late spring, followed by edible blue berries. Plant 45–60cm/ 18–24in apart for hedges 120cm/4ft upwards.

Opposite page: The diverse environment of a traditional country hedge.

The brown hairstreak, which lays on blackthorn, has suffered a dramatic decline in the last decades as hedges have been flailed and blackthorns ripped out by farmers who fear their spread. It is not the most dramatic of our native butterflies, but it is a part of the web that makes up the ecosystem and no-one knows what other species may be affected by its disappearance.

The value of hedges as a wildlife resource and as a part of the national heritage is now widely accepted, and subsidies are now available in parts of northern Europe for planting and maintaining hedges. But neither subsidies nor preservation laws can force farmers to maintain their hedges and, even now, it is still a battle to overturn decades of decline as existing hedgerows become overgrown and derelict even if new ones are, thankfully, being planted.

I am very fortunate to live in a part of the countryside where hedges still proliferate, and the majority are well tended, as this is stock country and nothing is as good – or as long-lasting – as a well-maintained thick and thorny native hedge for keeping sheep where they should be. My own garden is bordered on one side by an old holly hedge and on two more by an immensely varied hedge, predominantly hawthorn *(Crataegus monogyna)*, blackthorn *(Prunus spinosa)*, crab apple *(Malus sylvestris)*, damson *(Prunus domestica)*, guelder rose *(Viburnum opulus)* and hazel *(Corylus avellana)*. Among these are elders *(Sambucus nigra)* and brambles, with dog roses *(Rosa canina)* and honeysuckle *(Lonicera periclymenum)* threading through, as well as some non-native rambling roses which have escaped from the garden. Beneath it are primroses and bluebells, stitchwort, campion and foxgloves, meadowsweet, ragged robin, herb Robert and cow parsley, as well as garden escapees, such as crocuses and lungwort and masses of honesty and Solomon's seal; there are plantains, ribworts, buttercups and dandelions, deadnettles and all manner of grasses.

Amongst all of this live mice, voles and shrews, dozens of butterflies and insects plus so many birds that I can spend hours watching the activity in spring and summer. I also have a hunch that the horseshoe bats that swoop around on summer evenings enjoy the hedge, and last year a hedgehog hibernated in the thick protective undergrowth at one end. But I know I am privileged here, my hedge is one tiny link among thousands in the region which provide homes and pathways for creatures large and small. And if something terrible happened that meant I had to uproot my lovely old hedge, it would be a sad loss of diversity but would probably not have a serious impact on wildlife colonies in this area. However, this is definitely not the case in so many other places, where the decision to plant and maintain a hedge may be a crucial factor in the survival or disappearance of certain creatures.

HEDGING PLANTS

Berberis thunbergii 'Atropurpurea'
Tough, deciduous, very prickly
hedging plant with green or
purple leaves, turning bright red
in autumn. Masses of small
yellow flowers in spring, followed
by red berries. Shade tolerant.
Plant 45cm/18in apart for hedges
90cm/3ft upwards.

Buxus sempervirens (**common
box**) Dense, slow-growing, native
evergreen shrub with small, dark
green, glossy leaves. Shade
tolerant. Excellent for low hedges.
Plant 15–25cm/6–10in apart for
hedges 30–90cm/1–3ft high.

Buxus sempervirens
'Elegantissima' A variegated form
of common box. Leaves have a
creamy white margin. Suitable for
a compact hedge or as a specimen
shrub.

Carpinus betulus (**hornbeam**)
Hardy native plant similar to
beech. Suitable for shady and wet
positions. Keeps brown dead
leaves during the winter. Plant
25–45cm/10–18in apart for
hedges 90cm/3ft upwards.

Chaenomeles japonica (**flowering
quince**) Spiky hedging plant with
bright orange flowers in early
spring, followed by yellow
fragrant fruits in autumn. Can be
used as a wall shrub. Plant
45cm/18in apart for hedges
90cm/3ft high.

As well as nurturing so many different creatures, hedges are not only important as habitats per se, they are also vital in preserving biodiversity through their role as wildlife corridors, offering safe passage for a host of creatures creeping between other hedges, shrubberies and remnants of woodland habitat. This is especially important in built-up areas, where your garden hedge may not support as diverse a range of resident species as a hedge surrounded by other hedges, trees and shrubs, but it will provide perfect cover and shelter for visitors and migrants. Where habitats are rather isolated you will not get the wide range of creatures that come when they are closely linked, but you will provide vital sanctuary and support to ensure the survival of certain species in urban areas. In once rural areas hedges can be very important, connecting remnants of woodland habitat. In fact you may even see this within one garden, where a stretch of hedge will act as cover linking different areas. As wildlife populations in the countryside continue to be threatened by some agricultural practices, this role becomes more and more crucial.

Native hedges

Wherever we garden, we need to plant and maintain more hedges. There is a huge choice of useful species which set the style for a hedge, so you could go for a fairly formal hedge, one that is tall or short, or even a rather lax and wild look. Hedges can be highly ornamental, providing a progressively changing landscape, and while a fence is static, a typical hedge changes dramatically with the seasons – from the stark outlines of winter, through bright new shoots and blossoms in spring, to verdant foliage in summer and extraordinary diversity in autumn.

Although traditionally a feature of the countryside, mixed native hedges transfer well to most suburban situations. They are perfect for any reasonable sized garden, and can even be used in a very limited space. However, in that situation, or where the hedge is planned to border a formal area of garden, you may want to choose alternative hedging. Of course a mixed native hedge does not have to be a tall jumble, you can keep its subjects quite trim, at about 1.5m/5ft or so. You can also follow the traditional cottage gardeners' example and include one or two ornamental specimens, such as the gloriously scented early summer-flowering *Philadelphus lemoinei*, or the purple or white lilac *(Syringa vulgaris)*. Roses are a good accompaniment to a mixed hedge, the traditional mix would have almost always included dog roses; however, you may prefer to plant a favourite rambler or climber to romp through the foliage – just be sure to choose one that is not too fussy about pruning.

If the bulk of your hedge is made up of British natives you will benefit from a wonderful array of blossoms in spring, thick, dense, leafy greens in summer and coloured foliage from late summer to early winter. There will also be hordes of berries, until they are stripped for food. You can have a very diverse hedge bottom, with dozens of wildflowers flourishing – primroses and cow parsley, bluebells, red campion and dog's mercury – along with native grasses and climbing plants, which will twine through the hedging shrubs and trees.

A typical native hedge in spring will be filled with shoots of different colours, frothy clouds of blossom from hawthorn, blackthorn, and perhaps damson and crab apple, willow and hazel catkins – all of which provide early pollen and nectar – and pale green and coloured shoots of beech and dogwood. In summer the hedge will be a riot of different shaded foliage, perhaps studded with fragrant blooms of honeysuckle and the ephemeral flowers of a dog rose or two, sprinkling their heart-shaped petals on the ground.

In autumn it could be thick with dense hawthorns dripping with liver-red berries that songbirds will harvest over the winter. Blackthorns will be hung with plump blue

Cornus sanguinea (**dogwood**) Dense shrub with red stems and white flowers in spring. Green leaves turning to red/orange autumn colour. Good in wet or dry soils. Plant 45–60cm/18–24in apart.

Cornus stolonifera 'Flaviramea' (**yellow stemmed dogwood**) Dense shrub with bright yellow/green stems and green leaves, most obvious in winter. Makes good contrast to red-stemmed cornus. Suitable for wet conditions. Plant 45–60cm/18–24in apart.

Corylus avellana (**hazel**) Fast-growing, native hedging plant. Yellow catkins in spring, followed by edible nuts in autumn. Plant 60cm/2ft apart for hedges 150cm/5ft upwards.

Cotoneaster simonsii Semi-evergreen, upright shrub with small, dark green leaves. Small white flowers in early summer, followed by large scarlet fruit. Suitable for shady positions. Plant 60cm/2ft apart for hedges 180cm/6ft upwards.

Opposite page: The fluffy seedheads of Old Man's beard or wild clematis provide food for finches and other birds.

HEDGING PLANTS

Crataegus monogyna (**hawthorn**) Fast-growing native thorny hedging plant with white, scented flowers in spring and red fruits in autumn. Dark green glossy leaves. Suitable for wet positions. Makes an ideal security hedge. Plant 25–30cm/10–12in apart for hedges 90cm/3ft upwards, or plant a second row 45cm/18in apart, staggered with the first row.

Elaeagnus ebbingei Fast-growing evergreen shrub with large leaves, silvery underneath. Small, scented white flowers in autumn. Small orange fruits in spring. Plant 45–60cm/18–24in apart for hedges 150cm/5ft upwards.

Escallonia Evergreen hedging shrub with glossy dark green leaves. Suitable for windy and seaside, but not cold, positions.

Escallonia 'Apple Blossom' Slow-growing variety with pink and white flowers.

Escallonia 'Donard Seedling' Fresh-pink buds opening white. Strong growing variety.

Escallonia illinita 'Iveyi' Strong growing, white flowering variety.

Escallonia var. *Macrantha* Red flowering variety.

sloe berries, there may be rose hips that moth caterpillars will have mined out for food, and others that field mice will strip bare in late winter for their seeds. Dogwoods and guelder rose will provide both berries and brilliantly coloured foliage, damsons and crab apples will droop with fruit, hazels will be festooned with nuts for squirrels and mice, and the occasional evergreen hollies will be bright with berries, on top of all of that beech and alder buckthorn will be dripping with seeds. There may still be some scarlet honeysuckle berries, and twists of spiralling stemmed red-berried bryony, with a generous dusting of the fluffy seeds of old man's beard or wild clematis. There will probably also be brambles offering food and superb cover for birds and small mammals, and ivy will be thick with buzzing insects and small birds. There really is nothing like a hedge!

Planting a mixed hedge

Always plant a mixed hedge with at least five species, including an evergreen for shelter in winter. This will provide a balanced habitat and food source for the widest range of birds, butterflies and bees. It is also best to plant the species in groups of three or four together for the most natural look. For a thoroughly mixed hedge a good choice is around 80 per cent of hawthorn, blackthorn and buckthorn, with beech, hazel and dog roses, the other 20 per cent being made up of guelder rose, field maple, wayfaring tree, spindle, crab apple and holly or yew. It may also be worth allowing some willow and privet to grow to a good height. This would provide for the maximum number of insects, moths and butterflies as well as birds and small mammals.

If your hedge is near woodland and other hedges, you are likely to find seedlings of elder shooting up before long, as well as sycamore and some bramble, honeysuckle and wild clematis. Try and remove the sycamore, as these tend to crowd out other species and their wildlife value is comparatively limited. You will also need to be fairly ruthless about keeping brambles under control, as these will strangle young shrubs and trees.

Mark out a trench 45cm/18in wide and at least 30cm/1ft deep for the length of your hedge, and set the plants 30–45cm/12–18in apart. If you have the space for a really dense hedge, double the width of your trench by planting a second row, staggered in a zigzag pattern. Use bare-rooted specimens rather than container-grown rootballs, and include plenty of compost as you backfill. Home-made compost is always the best choice, but if you do not have enough buy in compost, making sure it is peat-free, and add some manure. Water newly planted specimens thoroughly, and keep them well watered while they are getting established.

Depending on your choice, you may not even need to buy plants. If you choose hazel (*Corylus avellan*) or willow (*Salix* spp.*)* you need only stick a branch into the ground and it will quickly form roots. You can also easily propagate many native trees and shrubs from seeds. Collect seeds in the autumn and sow them into trays or pots of moist compost, then leave them in a shady place over winter, making sure they never dry out. Do not put them inside, as most tree seeds germinate best if they have been exposed to frost. Even if only a fraction of those you plant germinate, it is very satisfying – and free. Self-sown seedlings may also appear in your garden, either fallen from a mature tree or dropped by a bird or buried by a squirrel or mouse. These are usually easy to uproot and transplant.

Time spent preparing the ground is never wasted, so the wider the trench and the more compost you include the better. Be sure to remove weeds from the trench and immediately surrounding area as you will want to underplant with native wildflowers and grasses, and these will struggle to get established if there is too much competition. Allow the hedging plants a year before you start underplanting, then, if you want to be sure of getting everything off to the best possible start, use wildflower plugs rather than seed. Once your habitat is established you should benefit from wildflowers that appear without your intervention, blown on the wind or brought in by the creatures that will soon inhabit your hedge and hedge bottom.

Alternatives to mixed native hedging

A hedge with a mixture of predominantly native species is generally best for wildlife; however, it may not be appropriate for your garden. Different situations demand different solutions, and there are plenty of single species hedges that are also valuable habitats. Any tangle of stems and branches will offer nesting opportunities and protection to birds, although many species offer so much more.

If you have a boundary that gets a reasonable amount of sun, yet you only have room for a low hedge, privet is useful. Let it flower and its nectar will attract dozens of butterflies, then when all the nectar is gone it will bear small black berries that are much appreciated by birds, especially blackbirds. It flowers and berries best if it is kept quite short, so lots of plants will grow against and beneath it, making it a good choice for a small garden where space is limited.

Blackthorn and hawthorn are superb wildlife plants, providing nectar, food and shelter all year round. Each makes an attractive single species hedge, although you must have a bit of space if you choose thorn, as the best thorn hedges need to be planted in staggered rows and should be allowed to reach at least 1.5m/5ft tall. If you have

---

HEDGING PLANTS

Fagus sylvatica (**beech**) Native hedging plant with green leaves, turning orange in autumn. Shade tolerant. Retains dead leaves during winter months. Plant 25–45cm/10–18in apart for hedges 90cm/3ft upwards, or plant a second row 45cm/18in apart, staggered with the first row.

Fagus sylvatica f. Purpurea (**copper beech**) Native hedging plant with deep purple leaves turning orange/copper in autumn. Retains dead leaves through the winter. Plant 25–45cm/10–18in apart for hedges 90cm/3ft upwards, or plant a second row 45cm/18in apart, staggered with the first row.

Hippophae rhamnoides (**sea buckthorn**) Native fast-growing thorny plant with thin silver leaves. Bears orange berries in autumn. Extremely good for coastal positions. Plant 45–60cm/18–24in apart for hedges 150cm/3ft upwards.

Ilex aquifolium (**holly**) Native dense, prickly, evergreen hedging plant. Suitable in shade and in industrial and coastal areas. Red berries in winter on female plants. Plant 35–45cm/14–18in apart for hedges 90cm/3ft upwards.

room to plant a thorn hedge, you probably have the space to plant a mixed native hedge, which will be even more valuable. On the other hand, if you want to plant a protective barrier, a mixed thorn hedge cannot be beaten. An ornamental thorny hedge of berberis will also deter intruders and has considerable wildlife value, offering shelter to small mammals and birds and providing food from its flowers and berries.

Yew is, of course, a wonderful hedge – magnificent, long lasting and particularly valuable for birds, with its tasty berries, secure nesting possibilities and excellent shelter. People are often put off planting yew because of the belief that it takes a long time to reach maturity. However, this is a myth, as yew will shoot away fairly swiftly if you prepare the ground well before planting and give it copious amounts of manure and water while it is getting established. Besides, speed is not everything, after all, few of us would ever plant a single tree if we were worried about seeing it reach maturity.

One of the fastest growing hedging plants is Leyland cypress, but I would never advise anyone to plant this. It grows fast, too fast for most situations unless you are prepared to spend the time constantly trimming and pruning it once it has reached its required height. On top of the maintenance issues, leylandii is not even that attractive. It is an unnatural shade of green compared with most of the countryside, and is very greedy, supping up vast amounts of moisture and nutrients from the soil while giving nothing back, save deep shade in which nothing will grow. Admittedly it provides nesting opportunities for birds, such as greenfinches and blackbirds, and starlings and other birds will roost in it, but it is a very poor choice for a wildlife garden. If you want tall, clipped, evergreen hedges yew is a much better choice in every situation.

Holly is also a magnificent hedging plant, and attracts dozens of insects, birds and butterflies, as well as its namesake the holly blue, that feeds on holly and ivy. If you want a fairly formal look but do not want yew, holly is the best choice. It can be kept neat without detracting from its wildlife value, and you can allow some plants to grow taller than the rest of the hedge and then clip them into formal shapes – spirals, cones or triangles. If you want a low-growing evergreen hedge, box *(Buxus sempervirens)* is a good choice, but let it flower in spring to attract insects.

Beech and hornbeam are popular and valuable hedging plants, although some people do not like the way their dry, brown leaves hang on all winter. A mix of copper beech and beech can look very effective, particularly in spring with the combination of bright green and reddish bronze leaves. These plants look most effective placed in slightly random blocks, rather than a symmetric pattern, which can look contrived in all but a formal setting. Even a large tree, such as oak, can be used in a hedge. The secret is to coppice it to keep it low and to promote bushy cover, rather than allowing it to reach for the sky.

Opposite page: A berberis hedge provides berries and shelter, and keeps cats away from nesting birds.

Below: Blackbirds will take black berries before any other colour.

HEDGING PLANTS

Ilex alternifolia 'Golden King'
Broad gold variegated leaves.
Female, so needs male hollies to
berry in winter. Good in shady
positions. Plant 45cm/18in apart
for hedges 90cm/3ft upwards.

Ilex aquifolium 'Argentea
Marginata' (**silver edged holly**)
Glossy leaves with creamy white
margin. Female, so needs male
hollies to berry in winter. Plant
35–45cm/14–18in apart for
hedges 90cm/3ft upwards.

Lavandula (**lavender**)
Evergreen edging plant with
narrow grey leaves and fragrant
flowers in summer. Prefers a
sunny position.

Lavandula angustifolia 'Hidcote'
Compact variety, violet flowers in
early July.

Lavandula angustifolia 'Munstead'
Compact form, lavender blue
flowers in early July.

Ligustrum vulgare (**privet**)
Native semi-evergreen hedging
plant with dull green leaves and
strongly scented white flowers in
July. Bears black fruit in winter,
ideal for birds and wildlife. Shade
tolerant. For planting distance see
Ligustrum ovalifolium.

You do not need to rule out non-native species entirely. Laurel *(Prunus lauroceasus)* has become rather unpopular because of its associations with municipal planting and gloomy nineteenth century shrubberies. However, give it its head and it can make a glorious, glossy evergreen hedge. Its creamy scented flowers are rich in nectar in spring, and the fat juicy black berries in late summer prove irresistible to blackbirds. Other good candidates are the Pyracanthus species and berberis, which knot together well to form a thick hedge, giving good cover and plenty of fruit and nectar. A hedge of *Rosa rugosa* provides a thorny barrier, excellent cover and produces attractive white or deep red flowers, followed by magnificent crops of stunningly generous hips in autumn. Escallonia is very useful in coastal districts, as it survives salty spray and wind and grows on very thin soil. It provides shelter and nesting sites, and feeds some insects, but is not otherwise valuable for wildlife. Rosemary is a good insect attractant hedge and also thrives near the coast, although it offers no shelter.

Hedge maintenance

To shape a hedge, begin pruning when plants are young to encourage uniform bushy growth. When you plant, cut young deciduous trees or shrubs back to about 15–20cm/6–8in from the ground. The next season trim off about half the new growth, and in the third year do the same. Ornamental hedges of lavender or rosemary only need light trimming to shape them and encourage flowering. Evergreen container-grown stock should not be cut back severely when planting, instead leave a year or two before trimming lightly to begin shaping.

The time you prune hedges is crucial. You can trim hedges in late summer after nesting birds have fledged their young, or late winter, although yew and other evergreens should be trimmed in late summer, allowing time for some new growth before the winter weather. Leave fruit- and berry-producing plants until late winter, when all the food will have been eaten but when they are still dormant, and beech and oak should be left until early spring, when the previous year's leaves should have dropped. Privet and box can be trimmed in late summer and again in spring, but allow them to flower to feed insects and butterflies.

If you inherit a large, overgrown, bare-bottomed and misshapen hedge, or even a badly pruned, thin and leggy young hedge, you should not despair. An old hedge can be resurrected if it is cut back in early spring to around 30cm/1ft below the desired height. Carefully trim it for the next few years to give it the desired shape and fullness. You can be really ruthless with a young hedge and cut it back to near ground level in early spring. Most deciduous hedging plants will happily tolerate this treatment and

Above: The hips of hedging rose *Rosa rugosa* are dramatically ornamental.

Opposite page: Holly is an excellent wildlife plant that responds well to trimming into formal shapes.

regrow with much sturdier and bushier growth, and privet can be cut right back to the ground. Evergreens, however, need more careful handling. If any evergreen hedge, apart from yew, has got out of hand you will probably need to replace it, as evergreens do not like such drastic treatment. Yew, however, can be brought back from the brink with very severe lopping as it will sprout from old wood.

If you have ornamentals such as philadelphus in your hedge, you need to prune carefully. Always wait until after it has flowered, as it blooms on old wood the following year. Woody flowering plants can generally be rejuvenated by cutting a third of the stems right back, pruning a third to make them bush out, and leaving a third, but this is not always possible in a hedge.

Where practical you should cut hedges so they are narrower at the top than the base. This allows light to reach the whole of the hedge, encouraging an even spread of bushy growth, plus it makes it harder for shade-loving ivy to establish itself, as well as encouraging a wider diversity of plants in the hedge bottom. This shape also reduces the risk of snow settling on top and damaging plants. You need to keep an eye on ivy

Below: Yew is the favourite choice for formal hedging, and valuable for birds and insects.

in a hedge. It should always be cleared from an old hedge as it can become a problem by strangling weaker plants, but if possible leave a few plants, as it is a valuable nectar producer.

Most hedges can be trimmed with a power trimmer once they are well established, although in the early years, when you need to be more selective, use a hand saw and secateurs. In mixed hedges you may initially need to chop back strongly growing species, such as field maple and hawthorn, harder than slightly less sturdy species, but as the hedge develops you can choose to trim it uniformly once a year or leave a few species to grow taller than others.

If a rural country hedge gets out of hand, it is traditional practice to rejuvenate it by laying it to encourage new growth and make it stronger, and if you inherit a very tall, thin hedge this is the most effective way of restoring the habitat. Hedge laying involves splitting the upright stems of existing shrubs, bending them horizontally along the length of the hedgerow and pegging them taut with stakes (made from pruned hedge material), a set distance apart. These vertical stakes give the finished hedge its strength, and if hazel stems are woven around their tops the hedge can be made even more formidable. Hedge laying is more a matter of traditional good practice than of particular wildlife value, but it is good for wildflowers as it opens up the hedge bottom.

Climbing cover

Climbing plants can provide many of the benefits of trees but have the added bonus of being space-saving, as they can be grown up fences and walls. Climbers provide sheltering sites for insects and spiders, nesting and roosting sites for birds, they may provide cover and safe corridors for small mammals, as well as producing beautiful flowers and fruit to boot. Honeysuckle is one of the best climbers of all. It is an indispensable plant for moths and butterflies, a magnet for many other insects, and it provides the tangled twisted stems that nesting birds love, along with autumn fruits. Its scent and habit makes it equally attractive to gardeners, and it has been rightly popular in gardens ever since the earliest cottagers used it to cover outhouses or mask the less pleasant odours of everyday life.

One of the most stunning examples of walls completely covered with creeping and climbing plants for wildlife cover is the home of the great British conservationist Miriam Rothschild. When you first arrive at her house, having followed a long rutted drive through a sea of cow parsley and wildflowers, it is hard to believe that you have come to the right place. The house, in the middle of a majestic wood, bordered by open countryside, is so completely covered by creepers that it looks abandoned. But this

HEDGING PLANTS

Malus sylvestris (**crab apple**) Native tree or shrub with pale pink flowers in spring, followed by red-flushed small green crab apples in autumn. Plant 35–45cm/14–18in apart.

Philadelphus 'Virginal' (**mock orange**) Vigorous hedging shrub suitable for dry positions, with fragrant double white flowers. Suitable for sun or shade. Plant 45cm/18in apart for hedges 150cm/5ft in height.

Photinia fraseri 'Red Robin' An evergreen shrub with dark green glossy leaves. New, young growth appears as a brilliant red, which makes this shrub a popular eye-catching choice.

Prunus laurocerasus (**common laurel**) Excellent dense, evergreen hedging plant with large, glossy green leaves. Good in shade. Plant 45–60cm/18–24in apart for hedges 1.2–6m/4–20ft in height. Prune hedge with secateurs in spring or late summer.

Prunus spinosa (**blackthorn**) Native dense, prickly hedging plant covered with masses of small white flowers in early spring. Sloe berries in autumn. Excellent dense thorny hedging shrub. Plant 35–45cm/14–18in apart for hedges 90cm–2.1metres/ 3–7ft in height.

HEDGING PLANTS

HEDGING PLANTS

Pyracantha (**firethorn**)
Dense, prickly, fast-growing
evergreen plant. White flowers in
early summer, colourful berries in
autumn. Good in shade and in
north and east facing positions.
Plant 45–60cm/18–24in apart for
hedges 120cm/4ft. Good as a wall
shrub or as a free growing
hedging plant.

Pyracantha gibbsii 'Golden
Charmer' Vigorous variety with
glossy green leaves. Fruits are
orange-yellow in colour.

Pyracantha gibbsii 'Mohave'
Medium sized variety, produces
deep green leaves and a profusion
of orange-red fruits.

Pyracantha gibbsii 'Orange Glow'
Vigorous variety, which produces
a bright orange-red berry lasting
well into the winter.

Rhamnus cathartica
(**common buckthorn**)
Large native shrub or small tree
suitable for hedgerows. Branches
are spiny. Small yellow flowers in
May, followed by masses of
shining black fruits in autumn.
Good on chalky soils. Plant
60cm/2ft apart for hedges
150cm/5ft upwards.

Opposite page: Clematis, wisteria
and ivy cover the walls of
conservationist Miriam
Rothschild's house.

rampant foliage is not due to any loss of control, indeed it was a deliberate choice to clothe the house to provide homes and food for as many creatures as possible.

The walls are covered with a carefully thought-out jumble of climbing and self-clinging plants. There are roses, wild and cultivated, mixed with quince, lilac, plum trees, ivy, Virginia creeper and clematis. Buddleia has grown straight upwards to bring butterflies round the bedroom windows. There is towering broom, wisteria, old man's beard, laurel, cherry trees and laburnum. Everything twists and scrambles up the walls and on to the roof, and the whole selection droops with flowers in late spring and summer, becoming a mass of hips and seedpods in autumn. Dozens of birds – from wood pigeons to goldcrests, fly-catchers to blackbirds – feed and nest there, bats swoop in and out at night, and all summer long clouds of butterflies, bees and other insects flit among the flowering plants. Buddleias, lilacs and broom are not usual subjects for walls, but Miriam discovered by chance that they will grow to a considerable height when planted against a wall among competition in their search for the sun. All add to the diversity.

The joy of climbers is the opportunity they give to create comparatively wide diversity in a comparatively small area, and there are subjects for any situation. Poor ivy is one of the underdogs in the plant world, seriously underrated by so many gardeners, who consider it rather beneath them. Yet it will grow happily in rubbish soil in a shady corner where little else will thrive, and it provides thick cover and a mass of pollen and little berries, all of which are incredibly alluring to insects as well as many small birds. Ivy is a favourite nesting place for wrens, and in a sunny spot it is indispensable for one of our garden butterflies, the holly blue, as it is one of this butterfly's main food plants. At the end of summer ivy will be completely thick with bees feasting on its late pollen. If that were not enough, it is also a very attractive plant, and if you find the glossy, evergreen dark green leaves too sombre, there are showy varieties with gleaming golden and silver splashes or borders to the leaves. Add to this the bonus that ivy grows vigorously, each new shoot can put on several feet of growth a year, it is self clinging and thrives happily without intervention, and it is hard to see why it is so neglected. Ivy has suffered from its reputation as house-wrecker, as its clinging tendrils will pierce crumbling mortar and pull old stone or brickwork to pieces, but if your walls are in good condition it will not affect them, in fact it will provide a useful layer of living insulation.

Any climber that happily colonises a cold north wall or a shady place is particularly valuable in a garden, especially a small garden where there may be little opportunity to create a wide range of habitats. Along with ivy, *Hydrangea petiolaris* is a classic

HEDGING PLANTS

Rhamnus frangula (**alder buckthorn**) Large native shrub or small tree with rounded leaves turning yellow in autumn. Fruits start red then turn black in winter, which attracts wildlife. Plant 60cm/2ft apart for hedges 150cm/5ft upwards.

Rosa arvensis (**field rose**) Native rose, excellent for hedgerows, with long slender stems. Large white flowers in July, followed by dark red fruit.

Rosa canina (**dog rose**) Native thorny rose with fast-growing arching branches. Large white to pink scented flowers in early summer, with red glossy fruit in autumn. Excellent for hedgerows.

Rosa multiflora A vigorous variety that will produce a spectacular effect if placed to ramble into nearby trees. Fragrant white flowers are followed by small fruit, which will last into the winter months. Ideal for hedging or use to cover any unattractive parts of your garden!

Rosa 'Roseraie de l'Hay' An excellent hedging rose of vigorous habit. Producing fragrant, deep red/purple double flowers with cream stamens.

HEDGING PLANTS

Rosa rubiginosa (**sweet briar/eglantine**) Native medium sized rose with dense prickly upright stems. Very aromatic leaves and clear pink fragrant flowers in June, followed by red fruits in autumn. Plant 30–45cm/12–18in apart for hedges 150–210cm/5–7ft.

Rosa rugosa 'Rubra' or 'Alba' (**hedging rose**) Large wine red or white, fragrant flowers during the summer months, followed by huge red hips in early autumn. Plant 30–45cm/12–18in apart for hedges 120–180cm/4–6ft and upward.

Rosa spinosissima (**Scotch rose**) Small native dense rose with tiny prickles. Small fragrant creamy flowers in late spring to early summer, followed by maroon/black fruit in autumn. Suitable for light soils. Plant 45cm/18in apart for hedges 60–90cm/2–3ft in height.

Rosmarinus officinalis (**rosemary**) Evergreen dense hedging shrub with aromatic grey/green leaves and light blue flowers in early summer. Makes excellent informal hedge. Requires a sunny position. Plant 35–45cm/14–18in apart for hedges 60–90cm/2–3ft.

Santolina incana
(**cotton lavender**) Low-growing, aromatic evergreen plant with silver foliage with yellow pom-pom flowers in July. Plant 30–35cm/12–14in apart for hedges 30–45cm/12–18in in height.

Symphoricarpos albus
(**snowberry**) Strong growing hedging plant suitable for shady positions. Clusters of small pink flowers in summer are followed by pure white berries in autumn and winter. Plant 45cm/18in apart for hedges 120–150cm/4–5ft.

Taxus baccata (**yew**) Magnificent long-lived evergreen hedging plant, producing bright red berries in late summer. Plant 45–60cm/18–24in apart for hedges from 120cm–4m/4–13ft.

Ulex europaeus (**gorse**)
Spiky native shrub with dense dark green shoots. Yellow flowers in spring. Prefers dry sunny positions and poor soils. Plant 45cm/18in apart for hedges

climber for a north-facing wall. It is very unfussy about soil and upkeep and once it gets established it will romp away, although it can take three or four years to feel at home. It is covered with panicles of pollen-rich white flowers in summer and although it loses its leaves in winter they first turn a myriad of glorious reddish hues.

The morello cherry (*Prunus cerasus* 'Morello') is another good candidate for a north wall, though it needs slightly richer soil than ivy or hydrangeas. Train this tree flat against the wall and you will be rewarded with swarms of birds and insects, which swoop towards its blossom on sunny days and then return for its late summer fruits, which hang on the tree for longer than sweet cherries, as they are very sour. You might consider planting blackberries on a wall to provide late summer food for insects and birds as well as yourself, but if you want to keep these under control choose the domesticated variety.

The most inviting climbers for sunnier walls are the butterflies' and moths' favourites, honeysuckle, and summer-flowering jasmine. The incomparably fragrant

Above: You may need to net grapes to beat the birds to them.

Opposite page: A well-trained fig provides dense cover and home for many insects.

jasmine is one of the best climbers of all to attract moths. Its scented white flowers shine out like a beacon to attract them on warm evenings, and its perfume is just as irresistible to humans. As far as nesting opportunities go, the tangling stems of clematis provide superb cover. The spring flowering *Clematis montana*, which sprinkles clouds of faint almond scent around the garden from its abundant blossom, is particularly popular with bees and other insects, while the native clematis, travellers' joy or old man's beard, flowers less dramatically but is worth growing for its rampant habit and trails of red berries, as well as the great clouds of fluffy seedpods that finches and other birds adore. Many clematis have very decorative seedpods as well as adorable flowers, but travellers' joy is the best choice for wildlife.

Wisteria blooms are so generous that they are the favourites of many insects and butterflies, and the plant's vigorous twining habit makes it another safe and attractive habitat for nesting birds. Roses, of course, are wonderful value, particularly those with generous hips, which support insects, spiders and field mice as well as birds, although roses are not butterfly plants as they do not produce nectar.

Grapevines may bear bunches of tempting fruit, and you can train many fruit trees flat against warm walls, bringing in numerous insects and birds. Fig trees are particularly exciting to a wide range of insects, although if you have limited space always choose a climber that will provide cover and shelter as well as nectar and fruit. Plants such as pyracantha or cotoneaster can be trained as wall shrubs, and flowering quince is another popular wildlife choice – with its pollen-rich flowers, prolific fruits and tangled growth habit.

Try to plant climbers 30–45cm/12–18in away from the wall, as the base of any wall tends to be very dry and rather infertile. You should dig the hole at least twice as deep as the required planting depth, then backfill half of it with rich compost or a manure and compost mix, and take particular care to keep climbing plants well watered. Where you need to erect a framework – which can be as simple as a few wires on vine eyes – to train climbers along, place your wires, trellis or frame several centimetres away from the wall to allow plants room to twine and also to ensure that wildlife has a sanctuary and corridor between the plant and the wall. Birds and bats particularly need this cover in urban areas or where there are cats nearby. The other thing you need to remember is to take care with pruning. Books might suggest you prune in summer as soon as possible after flowering, but be patient as fledglings may not yet have flown the nest, and if you expose them too early the parent birds may abandon them, and cats or other predators will have easy access. Also never prune a living wall too heavily, instead leave as much cover as you can.

HEDGING PLANTS

120–150cm/4–5ft in height. *Viburnum lantana* (**wayfaring tree**) Large native shrub with large leaves, hairy beneath. White flowers in early summer are followed by red fruits in autumn. The leaves produce a good autumn colour. Suitable for chalky soil. Plant 45cm/18in apart for hedges up to 2.1m/7ft in height.

Viburnum opulus (**guelder rose**) Vigorous native shrub with flat clusters of fragrant white flowers forming in early summer. Red berries follow these in autumn. Suitable for damp positions. Plant 45cm/18in apart for hedges up to 3m/10ft in height.

BEST CLIMBERS FOR WILDLIFE

Clematis vitalba (**wild clematis/old man's beard**)
Hedera helix (**ivy**)
Jasminum officinale (**jasmine**)
Lonicera periclymenum (**honeysuckle**)
Parthenocissus quinquefolia (**Virginia creeper**)
Rubus (**bramble**)
Wisteria sinensis (**wisteria**)

Opposite page: Luminous scented jasmine attracts butterflies and moths.

6 Flowery meadows and lawns

One of the many joys of living in a rural part of Britain is the wildflowers, the way they spring up to greet you on the first bright days. First come little yellow primroses heralding the spring, closely followed by clumps of bright marsh marigolds and clouds of stitchwort, cowslips, bluebells and, if you are lucky, fritillaries and orchids. Then lady's smock, vetches and all the wayside flowers of hedge bottoms and grassy verges appear.

As a child I could name more than ninety different wildflowers – apart from grasses – growing near my school in a valley a short hop from the Yorkshire moors. It is unlikely that I would be able to find so many today. Wildflowers have suffered an alarmingly high casualty rate over the past four or five decades, caused by roaring urbanisation and building, changes in farming practices and land management, and the persistent use of chemicals. As the wildflowers disappear, so too do the insects that seek them out, and the birds and creatures that prey on the insects – and so on. Butterflies are particularly at risk. The newer incursion of genetically modified crops with built-in herbicides poses another threat, if some of these organisms spread they could easily wipe out fragile communities of wildflowers.

It is a shocking statistic that 98 per cent of wildflower meadows in Britain have been lost since the 1940s. However we should not despair, as there is a lot that gardeners can do to help. While a garden can never be a substitute for the countryside, it is amazing what wildflowers will appear if you stop your weekly mowing routine and allow a patch of lawn to grow longer. In fact you can create a mini-meadow in just a few metres of garden. A wildflower meadow is an incredibly attractive feature and there is something unremittingly romantic about an area of soft grassland studded with colour, with clumps of flowers waving their heads at different heights above the grass, and others creeping along near ground level. Such a meadow in summer will be buzzing with insects and butterflies, chirping with grasshoppers, and full of scuttling mice and voles. You will probably send skylarks heavenwards as you wander past, and if you take the time to lie among the flowers and grasses and stare at the ground, you will see hundreds of different crawling and scuttling insects going about their business. There is no doubt about it, an established wildflower meadow is a stunningly diverse and attractive habitat.

Of course you will not get such a diversity in a garden meadow, as some wild plants rely on farm animals to create the optimum conditions for their survival and spread.

They may need the selective grazing and manuring of certain types of cattle, the mowing and weed control of sheep, or even a good trample by livestock at certain times of year. However with judicious planting and management you can create a pretty good imitation of a real wildflower meadow.

Choose between a traditional long-season meadow, a spring or summer meadow, or opt for an annual cornfield-style meadow, depending on the management of the rest of your garden. The simplest step is just to leave patch of grass to grow long – a strategy that works on any scale, whether in an open lawn, a grassy orchard or a specially allocated patch of garden. Wildflowers will soon appear, with all the benefits they bring.

The problems with modern grassland

Most grassland today is intensively grazed rye grass, rather than the mixed native grasses awash with wildflowers that were once grown for hay. Rye grass supports comparatively few species, and also crowds out native gasses and other plants, but it is fast-growing and gives a heavy yield. This makes it attractive for intensive farming, which, unfortunately means that modern agricultural grasslands have very poor wildlife value. And as the variety of plant species that can grow is so limited, the only wild herbivores such fields attract are those which like eating the intensive grass species. Even the insect and butterfly species that feed on grass cannot survive on modern grasslands, because the grasses are usually the wrong species.

The other problem is that modern harvesting or grazing regimes have such an effect on the habitat that relatively few small mammals, insects or butterflies can survive. Intensive grasslands are either grazed heavily from late spring or cut for silage, which is harvested much earlier in the year than hay. This leaves invertebrates with no time to complete their life cycles and ground nesting birds with no opportunity to raise their young. Few species can survive this rapid change or complete their lifecycle within the available period. Ground nesting birds and certain butterfly species are particularly vulnerable. Wild partridge and game birds are increasingly rare, and the corncrake, once a fairly common grassland bird, has almost vanished, while dozens of species of grassland butterflies are in peril.

Leaving aside this inhospitable management, modern grassland supports very little food for wildlife compared with traditional meadows. For example, a 1 acre/4ha traditional flowery hay meadow can support about two and a quarter million spiders, and all the insects they need to consume! Mixed grasses, flowers and weeds support thousands of invertebrates, from aphids to ladybirds, predatory soldier beetles, and

MEADOW GRASSES:

Agrostis canina (**Brown bent**)
Agrostis capillaris (**Common bent**) (**Chewing's fescue**)
Alcopecurus pratensis (**Meadow foxtail**)
Anthoxanthum odoratum (**Sweet vernal**)
Avenula pubescens (**Downy oat-grass**)
Briza media (**Quaking grass**)
Cynosaurus cristatus (**Crested dog's-tail**)
Deschampsia flexuosa (**Wavy hair-grass**)
Festuca rubra (**Red fescue**)
Festuca ovina (**Sheep's fescue**) (**Fine bent**)
Holcus lanatus (**Yorkshire fog**)
Hordeum secalinum (**Meadow barley**)
Phleum pratense (**Timothy grass**)
Poa pratensis (**Smooth meadow-grass**)
Trisetum flavescens (**Yellow oat-grass**)

Opposite page: Spiders' webs adorning mixed meadow grasses.

Agrimonia eupatoria (**Agrimony**) Yellow, medium height. Flowers June to August. Suitable for an informal lawn/summer meadow.

Agrostemma githago (**Corn cockle**) Pink, medium height. Flowers May to August. Suitable for an annual/summer meadow.

Anthriscus sylvestris (**Cow parsley**) White, tall. Flowers April to June. Suitable for a spring meadow.

Anthyllis vulnerarias (**Kidney vetch**) Yellow, small to medium height. Flowers June to September. Suitable for a summer meadow.

Bellis perennis (**Daisy**) White, low growing. Flowers March to November. Suitable for an informal lawn.

Calendula arvensis (**Marigold**) Orange, medium height .Flowers June to August. Suitable for an annual/summer meadow.

Cardamine pratensis (**Lady's smock**) Pink/white, medium height. Flowers April to June. Suitable for an informal lawn/long season meadow.

Centaurea cyanus (**Cornflower**) Blue, tall. Flowers June to September. Suitable for an annual/summer meadow.

Centaurea nigra (**Common knapweed**) Purple, medium to tall. Flowers June to September. Happy on any soil. Suitable for an informal lawn/long season meadow.

many caterpillars – all important food sources for other insects, small mammals and birds. The wide range of seeds also provide food for seed-eating song birds such as goldfinches; large numbers of voles, shrews and mice thrive in fields and field edges of wildflower meadows, which may in turn be predated upon by kestrels, owls, stoats, weasels and foxes. The diversity of plants and living creatures feeds the soil which, in turn, feeds all the ants, centipedes, millipedes, slugs leatherjackets and groundbeetles that live in the organic debris that falls to the floor of the field. A traditional meadow is an expansive larder accommodating most tastes, and one of the joys of planting a wildflower meadow as a garden habitat is the speed with which it will be colonised by appreciative creatures.

The best sites for creating wildflower meadows are those with soil that is well-drained and low in nutrients. Many wildflowers thrive in these conditions, while persistent coarser perennial weeds, such as docks and thistles, find it difficult to compete. But you do not need these precise conditions to get results. Even leaving a small patch of lawn to go wild will bring the reward of an increase of insects and birds, such as blackbirds, thrushes, starlings and dunnocks, which will come to hunt for worms, insects and leatherjackets. Even green woodpeckers may visit, seeking their favourite food, ants.

Deciding what to grow

The best traditional grazing and hay-making land can be found wherever the soil is fertileloam or clay base as this near neutral soil will support the widest range of plant species and associated creatures. Fertile grassland typically contains clovers, buttercups, lady's smock, meadowsweet, vetches and trefoils, daisies and campions. Alkaline chalk grassland also makes excellent grazing land. Its thin free-draining soil nurtures fine grasses and a wide range of flowers that are particularly attractive to butterflies. You are likely to see cowslips, yellow rattle, yarrows, thistles, knapweed, hawkweed, scabious, restharrow and plantains, and maybe orchids. Similar flowers can be found on the thin limestone soil of many hilly areas, where harebells usually prosper, along with wild thyme. But other hilly areas have very thin acid soil and rough wet grassland – usually used for grazing sheep – where bracken, heathers and bilberries grow, along with bog-loving plants such as sedges, rushes and asphodel. This is known as acid heathland. You can introduce any of these grassland types and accompanying flowers into a garden, but it is always best to boost the prevailing local ecology. So look around you and see which wildflowers are flourishing in nearby verges, fields or wasteland, then buy seed containing similar species.

The cornfield meadow is a slightly different creature from the wildflower meadows of permanent grassland. While other meadows build up their diversity over years, a cornfield meadow is a more fleeting habitat as it is full of showy annuals – although most self-seed vigorously and will return the following year. Sunny, nectar-rich cornfield meadows are particularly valuable for bees and butterflies in the summer, and many of the flowers – cornflowers, poppies, corncockles – are equally at home in borders in the garden.

It is possible to include a wildflower meadow in any sized garden, just scale it down accordingly. A variety of species will appreciate even a tiny patch of grass, and wildflowers such as Queen Anne's lace, cowslips, coltsfoot and lady's smock will act as a bird and insect café and a butterfly pub. This small patch will shelter beetles and other ground dwelling insects, even if it is not big enough to act as a breeding haven for the grass dwelling butterflies that may feed there.

One novel solution to a lack of space for wildflowers and grasses is to cover a roof with meadow turf and sow or plant wildflowers into it. In Britain very few people have incorporated turf roofs into the design of their houses, although it is much more common in parts of Scandinavia, but there is no reason why you cannot cover a garden shed or studio with grass rather than just using roofing felt. The London Wildlife Trust has an inspiring example in an inner city garden where an old outside toilet is covered

Above: The turf roof of this simple German cabin is covered with wildflowers.

Opposite page: Once cowslips establish, they will spread vigorously.

with grasses and wildflowers, and the roof of the purpose-built wooden information centre is also planted with butterfly attracting plants. To cover a shed you first make sure there is adequate slope for drainage, as you do not want to end up with a heavy pond on the roof, next cover the roof with a strong waterproof membrane, lay some grit on top of this to help drainage, and then put poor soil on top of that. Plant or sow wildflowers and native grasses and watch the birds, insects and butterflies enjoy it.

Informal lawn

Any patch of wildflowers gracing a garden is a bonus, and the easiest way to introduce them is to create an informal flowery lawn. You can do this simply by leaving stretches of your existing lawn unmown and seeing what plants appear. If you have the space, mown paths between the long grasses and flowers look spectacular. In a small patch leave the grass to grow until May or June, then cut it regularly with your mower blades set on a high setting. Of course, whether you can leave sections of grass long for months at a time depends on how you use your garden.

What appears will depend on your soil, your site and on on the way you have gardened over the years. If you are starting with a lawn that has been well mown but not overmanicured, and which has not been exposed to weedkillers or other chemicals, you will probably find that quite a few flowers spring up in no time. These will increase and spread as the fertility of the soil decreases without the constant dressing of grass mowings and other attention. It is extraordinary how many flowers appear, and you will wonder where they came from. You may even find that rarities, such as orchids, appear from nowhere and spread. Of course they can just as easily disappear without warning – in fact it is the unpredictability of nature and the anticipation of the unexpected which becomes one of the delights of a more natural style of gardening. If you want more diversity, buy small wildflower plants (plugs) and insert them straight into the meadow area. Always buy native wildflowers, as foreign ones may be invasive and will not support the same range of wildlife as our natives.

If you have been keeping a billiard table type lawn for years, closely cropped and

Lathyrus pratensis (**Meadow vetchling**) Yellow, tall. Flowers May-August. Suitable for a summer meadow.

Leontodon autumnalis (**Autumn hawkbit**) Orange-yellow. Flowers July to October. Suitable for an informal lawn/long season meadow.

Leontodon taraxacoides (**Lesser hawkbit**) Yellow. Flowers June to October. Good on chalky soil and sand dunes. Suitable for an informal lawn/long season meadow.

Leucanthemum vulgare (**Ox-eye daisy**) White, medium to tall. Flowers May to September. Suitable for a spring/informal lawn/long season meadow.

Linaria vulgaris (**Yellow toadflax**) Yellow, medium to tall. Flowers June to September. Suitable for a summer/long season meadow/informal lawn.

Lotus corniculatus (**Birdsfoot trefoil**) Yellow, low growing. Flowers June to September. Suitable for a summer/long season meadow.

Lychnis flos-cuculi (**Ragged robin**) Pink, low growing. Flowers May to August. Likes damp soils. Suitable for a mid spring meadow.

Malva moschata (**Musk mallow**) Pink, medium height. Flowers July to August. Suitable for an informal lawn.

Matricaria chamomilla (**Corn chamomile**) White, medium height. Flowers May to September. Suitable for an annual/summer meadow.

well fertilised with weeds controlled by herbicides, and you decide to leave a patch to fend for itself, the results will be fairly unspectacular. You will probably become overwhelmed by what are considered common lawn weeds – dandelions, buttercups, daisies and low-growing rosette plants, such as plantains and cat's ear, among fast-growing predominantly rye grass. In such cases it is best to dig up the area of lawn that you want to go wild, and start from scratch, preparing the ground well. You must remove all perennial weeds, along with their roots, and resow in autumn with an informal lawn mixture of grass and wildflower seeds. Do not add any compost or fertilisers, as lack of fertility is the key, and wildflower seeds will be reluctant to give their best in ground that has been heavily fertilised and herbicided. To begin with you will probably get a fine display of lawn grasses along with the newly-sown natives, and you will need a great deal of patience, plus some faith, that diversity will increase year on year – again you can always add some plugs to speed the process.

Some people advise that before resowing you should strip off the existing turf, along with 5-10cm/2–4in of topsoil. They then recommend adding about 10 per cent sharp sand to the top soil before replacing it. However this is not really necessary, as a bit of patience and the right mixture will bring better results. Make sure that your mix contains a good proportion of the semi-parasitic annual yellow rattle (Rhinanthus minor), as this will discourage lawn grasses from coming through and will knock back any that do. It is a good idea to scatter some yellow rattle seed along the edges of your new wildflower meadow if it is in the middle of an existing lawn, as it is one of the few wildflower seeds that usually germinates successfully in closely cut grass, and it will restrain the vigour of the lawn grasses surrounding your wildflowers. There is little point, however, in scattering the seeds of other wildflowers over existing grass, as they are extremely unlikely to germinate under the competition of existing species.

Spring meadow

Many gardeners do not like long grass year round, particularly where space is limited, as they want to use grassy areas of a garden for recreation in summer. In this case a spring meadow is the best choice, as you can mow the grass after flowering is finished in July, allowing you to use it as a lawn throughout the summer. Spring meadow flowers include cowslips and bugle, speedwells and lady's smock, stitchwort and yellow rattle, and a spring meadow is the perfect habitat for spring bulbs, such as bluebell, daffodil, lesser celandine and snakeshead fritillaries.

You can create a spring meadow from your existing lawn simply by planting bulbs and a few pot-grown wildflowers, or you could sow a new patch. A spring bulb meadow is a good choice for fertile and reasonably moist soils, while most wildflowers do better in poorer conditions. There is a particular caveat when planting bulbs, be sure to plant the English native bluebell (*Hyacinthoides non-scripta*) and steer clear of the Spanish bluebell (*Hyacinthoides hispanica*), which is much more aggressive than its British cousin. This Spanish bluebell has escaped the confines of the gardens to which it was first introduced and has made its way into the wild, where it has crossbred promiscuously with English bluebells, putting these elegant natives at risk. However, there is nothing wrong with a sprinkling of other non-natives, and I particularly welcome patches of tulips and camassias in any spring meadow. It may not exactly be the natural look, but it is glorious.

Above: Kidney vetch is bright in a summer meadow.

Opposite page: Field poppies and corncockles are staples of an annual summer meadow.

Ononis repens (**Common restharrow**) Pink/purple, small plant. Flowers June to September. Good on well-drained soil. Suitable for a summer meadow.

Papaver rhoeas (**Corn poppy**) Red, tall. Fowers June to September. Suitable for an annual/summer meadow.

Primula veris (**Cowslip**) Yellow, short to medium height. Flowers April to May. Good on dry chalky soil. Suitable for a spring meadow.

Plantago lanceolata (**Ribwort plantain**) Green, low growing. Flowers April to October. Suitable for a long season meadow.

Prunella vulgaris (**Self-heal**) Violet-blue, low growing. Flowers June to November. Suitable for an informal lawn/long season meadow.

Ranunculus acris (**Meadow buttercup**) Yellow, medium to tall. Flowers April-September. Prefers damp soil. Suitable for an informal lawn/ foundation meadow.

Ranunculus bulbosus (**Bulbous buttercup**) Yellow, medium height. Flowers May to July. Good on all well-drained soils. Suitable for a summer/long season meadow.

Rhinanthus minor (**Yellow rattle**) Yellow, low to medium height. Flowers May to September. Suitable for an informal lawn/spring/long season meadow.

Opposite page: 'Farmers Nightmare' cornfield meadow mix was developed by Miriam Rothschild.

Summer meadows

A permanent summer meadow, full of butterfly favourites such as knapweeds, scabious and vetches, can be cut throughout the spring, after which time it should be left untouched from May until late September, when all species will have shed seed. Meadow grass must never be left to decompose on site after mowing, as it will add to the fertility of the meadow. Instead rake grass cuttings to the edge of the patch so that any caterpillars' eggs, chrysalises or cocoons have the chance of completing their lifecycles. Summer meadows do best on poor soils, otherwise coarser flowers and grasses tend to take over.

Long-season meadows

You can also create a long-season meadow, which flowers from spring to autumn, and which will include a range of spring and summer flowers and biennials. A long-season meadow should only be cut two or three times in spring, then left until the autumn seed crop has set. This means it will really work best as a stand-alone feature rather than as a part of your garden that you use for recreation.

When you are establishing a meadow the grass always seems a hundred times more vigorous than the flowers, and you may need to cut a large long-season meadow relatively often, otherwise you may end up with a huge heavy mat of cut grass to be raked off in summer, and a rain-sodden mass in autumn. If this is a problem, divide large areas of grass into smaller ones and cut these at different times. This staggered cutting regime imitates the way in which grassland used to be managed, when animals grazed different fields at different times of the year. Mow some areas continuously throughout the spring, and allow them the freedom to grow for two or three months after the end of May. Most common wild flowers, such as campions, knapweeds and ox-eye daisies, will cope with this early decapitation and will just flower a little later (in July and August), in grass of reduced height. These areas should then be mowed and kept relatively short throughout the autumn, so that the grass never really gets the upper hand. Other areas, however, can be sown with yellow rattle in the autumn and, with the grass considerably subdued, can be left uncut until July, after the rattle has dropped its seed (which will germinate the next spring).

Annual cornfield meadow

The annual cornfield meadow is perhaps the most visually brilliant of all wildflower meadows, and a paradise for butterflies. Lots of gardeners, seduced by photographs in books and the images on seed packets, have decided to create one of these meadow,

without realising that they are probably the most difficult meadows to establish and manage. Soil condition is particularly crucial here – annual wildflowers will not flourish unless they are given free draining, infertile soil, with minimal competition from perennial weeds or grasses.

But remember that a cornfield meadow is really only a collection of annual plants, so you can treat it like any other patch of annuals in your garden. The key is to sow the seeds in spring into well prepared, but impoverished, ground, then enjoy their summer blooms and watching them fade away in autumn. As with any other annuals, you have to resow each year for the best effect, although many will reseed happily. Never add compost or fertiliser to your annual cornfield ground, just turn the ground over as necessary and rake it well in spring.

Below: Cranesbill, wild geranium is a thoroughly garden-worthy plant.

Sowing a new permanent meadow

The best situation for the largest number of wildflowers is a well-drained, sunny site, but if that is not possible, you can make a meadow in all but the dampest and shadiest areas. You will just have to be sure that you choose the correct seed for the soil and site.

Prepare the area by digging, weeding, and raking – as if you were sowing an ordinary lawn. An informal grass mix should consist of about 95 per cent non-rye grass lawn seed, with the rest consisting of wildflower seeds. The mix will depend on your soil, and whether you want a spring or summer meadow. A spring mix will contain species such as birdseye speedwell, birdsfoot trefoil, daisies, cowslip, hawkbit, hawkweed, hoary plantain, horseshoe vetch, Lady's bedstraw, meadow buttercup, meadow pea, musk mallow, selfheal, yellow rattle and field scabious.

If you are only sowing a small patch of garden, you can probably purchase seed from your local nursery or garden centre, but otherwise it is best to go to a wildflower meadow specialist. Ask where the seed comes from, as there have been some concerns about sowing non-native flowers and grasses. Many of the best meadow mixes are harvested from ancient meadows that have been pastureland for well over a thousand years, and your supplier will give you a breakdown of the species present, and in what percentage. Of course some seeds, such as orchids, are so fine that they probably will not show up in any analysis, so you may get some pleasant surprises.

It is generally best to sow meadow seed thinly – your supplier will advise – no more than 4gm per square metre/$^1/_8$oz per square yard This is to prevent the stronger growing grasses overwhelming the slower germinating species. The exception is when you are making a flowery informal lawn on bare soil, then you can sow at around 30g per square metre/$^7/_8$oz per square yard

As wildflower and grass seeds tend to be very fine, it is a good idea to mix them with silver sand for weight. This ensures you get a more even spread as you broadcast them on the ground. The best time to sow is autumn, as some wildflower seeds need the cold of winter to germinate. Of course some may be reluctant even then – cowslip seeds in particular can be very slow to appear, few raising their heads for four years or more. If this is a problem then you could plant them as plugs. Firm the area you have sown firmly, and water it well, and you should have a reasonable display the year following an autumn sowing, with diversity increasing each year.

In the first year after sowing you should keep any meadow well mown to encourage the grasses to spread and cover the ground, carefully raking off all clippings to keep fertility low. Start your spring or summer meadow mowing regime when your meadow has had a year to establish itself.

BRITISH WILDFLOWER SEEDS FOR MEADOWS AND INFORMAL LAWNS

Rumex acetosella (**Sheep's sorrel**) Green/pink, low growing. Flowers May to August. Suitable for a summer meadow.

Sanguisorba minor (**Salad burnet**) Red, medium height. Flowers May to September. Suitable for a spring/long season meadow.

Sanguisorba officinalis (**Greater burnet**) Red, tall. Flowers June to September. Suitable for a summer/long season meadow.

Scabiosa columbaria (**Small scabious**) Blue, low to medium height.Flowers July to August. Prefers dry chalky soils. Suitable for an informal lawn/summer meadow.

Stellaria graminea (**Lesser stitchwort**) White, tall. Flowers May to October. Suitable for a spring/long season meadow.

Tragopogon pratensis (**Goat's-beard**/Jack-go-to-bed–at-noon) Pale yellow, medium height. Flowers June to July. Suitable for a summer meadow.

Trifolium pratense (**Red clover**) Pink, low growing. Flowers May to September. Suitable for a summer/long season meadow.

Veronica chamaedrys (**Birdseye speedwell***) Blue, low growing. Flowers March to August. Suitable for an informal lawn.

Vicia cracca (**Tufted vetch**) Blue-purple, tall. Flowers June to August. Suitable for a summer/long season meadow.

7 Ponds and wetlands

If you only make one change to your garden to make it more wildlife-friendly, add a pond. Any permanent water, whether it is the size of a puddle or a substantial lake, or even just a marshy or boggy area, brings all sorts of creatures into your garden. You will create somewhere for residents and visitors to drink and bathe, and a breeding and feeding place for a whole host of pondlife – amphibians, invertebrates, insects, plus all the creatures that prey upon them. You may attract dragonflies, damselflies, frogs, toads, newts and hordes of insects and birds, as well as numerous water-dwelling creatures – water boatmen and pond-skaters will appear within hours of filling a pond.

As with other wildlife-friendly habitats, it is important to create more ponds to make up for the huge numbers that have been lost over the past century, with all the consequences for wildlife and diversity. Until the twentieth century, ponds were an important feature of the countryside. Almost every village and farm would have had one, and they were used as a source of drinking water, for watering animals and carriage horses, keeping fowl and fish, as well as for washing and as a focal point of village activity and play. As piped water became commonplace ponds gradually became less important for human activity, and their value as a diverse habitat was largely ignored.

Ponds are unstable environments, and if they are neglected they change form. They are prone to silting up and becoming overgrown, turning into bush-covered marshland or seasonal wetlands, and they may eventually end up as little more than dry land colonised by scrub trees and bushes, willows and alders – although it usually takes human intervention, such as draining or damming a watercourse, for them to degrade this far. Their very instability means they have huge potential for being reclaimed and turned into dry land, and many country ponds have been drained and turned back into farmland (or worse). Hundreds of village ponds have been emptied and the land used for building. Sadly, even where country ponds remain, the water is often polluted with chemical run-off from farmland, so aquatic life is limited.

Marsh and bog-land has suffered the same fate, endangered by the effects of drainage and agricultural pollution. Bogs and marshes are very fragile habitats, incredibly sensitive to pollution but supporting some of the rarest wildflowers and insects in the country. In the past fifty years more than half of Britain's lowland fens, for example, have been lost. Peat bogs have been additionally endangered through peat mining, and some of our most sensitive ecology has been destroyed to produce compost. Gardeners must avoid peat-

based composts, there are dozens of alternatives which do not destroy our environment.

Once there were scores of dew ponds in limestone or chalk country. These were shallow ponds of puddled earth that provided drinking water for cattle, made by hollowing out a bowl-shaped dip in the lowest part of the land and sending in the animals to trample the sides smooth, then waiting for dew (and rain) to fill the depression. Dew ponds are particularly interesting, because they have always been seasonal and largely dried out in summer, but are still valuable haunts for all sorts of insects and plants, and some amphibians. A wetland does not have to be completely wet all year round to provide an important habitat, and if an area of your garden is prone to flooding at certain times, do not be in too much of a hurry to drain it, you may instead be able to take advantage of its seasonal bogginess to provide a habitat for all sorts of flora and fauna that would not thrive elsewhere.

If you are creating an entirely new pond, you need to think carefully about what you want before you start – you are not going to be able to move it later. First of all, what wildlife do you want to attract, and what plant life do you want to grow? Even a tiny pond will bring in frogs and loads of insects, as well as all the creatures that come for the drinking water, although toads prefer a larger volume of water. Birds and bats will appear wherever there are insects for them to feed on – bats are particularly partial to the midges and mosquitoes that proliferate round water. Dragonflies need sunny ponds, preferably with a surface area of at least 4m/13ft square if they are to stay and breed, though they will visit much smaller ponds. Dragonfly larvae feed voraciously on tadpoles, so if you want to encourage dragonflies, be aware that you may end up with very few frogs.

Many aquatic plants are happiest in very shallow water, but most water lilies flourish best in a depth of around 80cm/32in, and if you are going to keep fish you need a minimum 60cm/2ft depth to prevent them suffering if the pond freezes. However, fish and wildlife are not an ideal combination, as fish will eat lots of other wildlife – newts, frog and toadspawn and dragonfly larvae, plus the organisms that help keep your pond clean and healthy. They also attract herons, which can be a problem in some large ponds in open situations. If herons are a nuisance, you need to stretch a couple of strands of wire near the edge of your pond, because the birds usually land near a pond and walk up to the edge.

The question of where to site your pond is important. If you have already got a damp or boggy patch, it is often tempting to transform this area into a fully-fledged pond; however, it may provide a perfect habitat just as it is, so is best left undisturbed. The main question is whether you can put a pond in sun or shade. A sunny stretch of

Opposite Page: A large pond near natural water may attract kingfishers and other riverside creatures.

SUBMERGED PLANTS

Callitriche stagnalis
(**common water starwort**)
Ceratophyllum demersum
(**rigid hornwort**)
Hottonia palustris (**water violet**)
Myriophyllum spicatum
(**spiked water-milfoil**)
Potamogeton crispus
(**curled pondweed**)

FLOATING PLANTS

Hydrocharis morsus-ranae
(**frogbit**)
Nymphae spp. (**water lilies**)
Polygonum amphibium
(**amphibious bistort**)
Potamogeton natans
(**broad-leaved pondweed**)
Ranunculus aquatilis
(**common water crowfoot**)
Ranunculus circinatus
(**fan-leaved water crowfoot**)

For smaller ponds choose
Nymphaea caroliniana 'Nivea'
N. froebeli
N. pygmaea

For ponds over 4m/13ft square
N. marliacea albida

For larger ponds
Nymphaea lutea
(**yellow water lily**)
Nymphoides peltata
(**fringed water lily**)

water will attract more wildlife and support more plants – as well as dragonflies, butterflies and insects, you may even get basking grass snakes on sunny lily pads. However, you also need plenty of shade at the margins and on the water to encourage many aquatic creatures to breed and shelter. A sunny but sheltered spot is the ideal, with a bit of shade on one side from shadow falling from a hedge or fence, or from large-leaved plants. And, of course, it is best if you can place a pond where it can be seen from the house or convenient sitting-out areas.

It is recommended not to site a pond under too many overhanging trees, mainly because of the problem the leaves cause when they fall in autumn. If too much leaf litter falls into the water it reduces its oxygen content and destroys aquatic life, so you will have to spend time carefully removing the leaves. Do this by hand or with a rake, taking care not to take up too much silt, as this is home to lots of pond inhabitants, including dragonfly larvae. On the other hand, water that is partially shaded tends to stay cooler and be better oxygenated, making it more suitable for pond creatures. It is also less liable to grow blanket weed or algae than a sunny stretch. A few trees and shrubs round the edge of the pond can enhance its value, they look attractive and provide perching places for birds – you may even get kingfishers and flycatchers.

The other important decision is whether you want still or moving water. Gently rippling and flowing water can make a very attractive feature in any garden, but still water is generally best for wildlife, and many plants – including water lilies – will not grow in moving water. One reason people want moving water is because it is easier to keep clean, and while this is true at the beginning as there is little opportunity for weed and algae to build up in fast-flowing wate, a properly managed still pond should stay clear without any help once it has built up the correct mix of organisms. Though a newly created pond may be a bit murky for the first couple of years, you should have no trouble after that, as long as you introduce appropriate planting. In the first two years you may need to be pretty assiduous in removing blanket weed and other algae, so that the organisms that naturally oxygenate the pond and keep it clean have the chance to develop, after that it should take care of itself and require nothing more than occasional weeding.

Making a wildlife pond

The key to a good wildlife pond is to have a gentle slope on at least one edge. This creates the warmer shallows and muddy margins that are invaluable for birds to bathe in and for frogs and other amphibians to spawn in. This shallow water is also preferred by many marginal aquatic plants, while the boggy area, where the gentle slope meets

dry land, is inviting for many of the whispering grasses and leafy plants which will provide cover for creatures entering and leaving the water. These plants also provide visual links between the pond and its surroundings. A gentle slope also means that any creature (or child) which falls into the pond has a better chance of clambering out, plus it makes pond cleaning easier. The only case where steeply shelving margins (with some 'escape ladder' for wildlife) may be acceptable is if herons pose a continual problem and are undeterred by a couple of strands of wire placed near the margins of the pond.

The best ponds have depths and shallows, clear water and water hidden and shaded by leaves or rocks. Different depths of water are important for vegetation and pondlife. Some plants need to sit with their feet in muddy water, others, including water lilies need to be planted in between 60–80cm/24–32in of water before they will flower. They will not grow in shallower water because of the very marked temperature changes that occur there. Some aquatic creatures are happy to slink or bask around boggy edges, others need to lay their eggs under deeper-rooting broad leaved plants, and some creatures and larvae need to live at the bottom of deep water.

An irregular shape always looks more natural than something geometric, but if your garden layout is rather formal, stick with the regular shape you want – the wildlife will not care! If a slope does not fit with the formality of your design, put a few rocks and stones at the edge of the pond to provide a shelf, and always place a log or piece of chicken wire in the pond as an exit for any creatures that fall in – hedgehogs are

particularly prone to falling into ponds when they drink.

The best time to make a pond is over the winter, when you will cause least disturbance to the wildlife in your garden. Making a pond at this time will also ensure it is ready to be colonised in spring, when aquatic creatures are looking for breeding sites. If your pond is built in winter, it also gives you the chance to let it fill up naturally with rainwater, rather than having to start off with tapwater. If you do have to use tapwater, you must leave it for at least a week before adding plants or wildlife, and always top up with rainwater once your pond is established – tapwater contains additives that disturb the balance of nutrients in your pond and may harm plants and wildlife. It will take longer for a pond filled with tapwater to clear and stay clear, as oxygenating plants will have to work harder, and pond-clearing organisms will take longer to build up.

Choices

There are four materials which you can use to make a pond – concrete, rigid pre-formed fibreglass liner, plastic liner, or clay. The simplest to install are those made from pre-formed fibreglass. This is a reasonably tough and durable material, and should last for many years, unless the water freezes solid in winter, which can cause cracking. All you need to do to fit an instant pre-formed pond is to dig a hole approximately the right shape, make sure it is level, drop in the liner and fill round the edges, before filling the pond and planting as appropriate. But this will not be an ideal wildlife pond, as it will not provide a friendly surface for plants and other pondlife, and it can take a while to blend into a garden, needing very careful planting to look either natural or inviting. On top of that, pre-formed fibreglass ponds come in a rather limited range of shapes.

If you are making a pool in solid ground with no risk of settlement you could build a concrete shell in any shape you wish, and this should last for decades if well made. You need to leave a concrete pond for several months after it is constructed, preferably over winter, before introducing plants or wildlife. This will allow it to weather and give the alkaline chemical residues in the cement time to become neutralised. Ideally you should fill and drain the pond two or three times before you introduce the final water, and leave that to settle for a week or two before you begin adding aquatic life.

Making a concrete pond is a methodical building job. You must make sure the ground is properly levelled and firm before you add the concrete, which should have waterproofing liquid incorporated into it. A sloping edge is doubly important with a concrete pond, as it ensures that if the water freezes it will slide up the edge rather than freezing into a solid block that could crack the concrete. For a large pond, it is a good idea to press some wire mesh into the first layer of wet concrete, then spread more on top of it. This reinforces the concrete, making it stronger as a large volume of water is a heavy weight, and it is quite hard to repair concrete ponds if they do crack under the strain.

Probably the easiest choice for most people is a flexible liner of polypropylene, PVC or butyl rubber. Flexible liners have the advantage of fitting almost any size and shape hole and are quick and fairly easy to use. The disadvantages are that they may break down due to weathering, and they can be punctured easily. But if you choose the best quality liner you can afford, and take care when laying it, you shouldn't have problems. Plastics do have a certain shelf life, so it's always advisable to buy the most expensive you can afford. A thick butyl liner should survive for well over a decade while cheap plastic may only last for a few years as it will degrade in sunlight, and is very susceptible to tearing. However, don't be put off from making a pond because your budget's limited, it isn't difficult to clear out a pond and lay another liner and the wildlife won't care what's holding the water.

Preparation is crucial when you're laying a flexible liner. When you have dug your pond to the size and shape you want, you need to make sure the sides are as smooth as possible as any stones or roots could puncture the liner. Ideally you should cover both the sides and base with a 5cm/2in layer of geotextile matting, or sand and carpet

MARGINALS

Alisma plantago-aquatica (**common water plantain**)
Aponogeton distachyos (**cape pondweed**)
Butomus umbellatus (**flowering rush**)
Equisetum fluviatile (**water horsetail**)
Iris pseudacorus (**yellow iris**)
Mentha aquatica (**water mint**)
Menyanthes trifoliata (**bogbean**)
Myosotis scorpioides (**water forget-me-not**)
Orontium aquaticum (**golden club**)
Ranunculus flammula (**lesser spearwort**)
Sparganium erectum (**branched bur-reed**)
Typha minima (**lesser reedmace**)
Veronica beccabunga (**brooklime**)

underfelt to prevent possible damage from small sharp stones. Estimate the length of liner you need by multiplying the deepest depth by two and adding the length of your pond. The width will be twice the average depth plus the pond's width. You also need to allow a good overlap of about 45cm/18in in all directions, for anchorage.

Lay the sheet methodically, smoothing it down as much as possible to make sure there are no air bubbles trapped underneath. Check that your boots do not have small stones embedded in the soles when you step on the liner – be aware of this as well when the pond is full and you are clearing it. In fact some people prefer to take their boots off altogether, but this is obviously a matter of personal preference as some of us are less keen than others on wading around in the sludgy sediment at the bottom of a pond. It is a good idea to weight the liner by carefully placing rocks at the deepest point, and do not trim the edges until the pond is completely full. You can hide the edge of the liner by digging a trench all round the pond and burying it, securing it well with soil. Alternatively, lay flat stones, tiles or slates on top of the liner on a bed of wet mortar. Arrange these so that they overhang the edge of the pond by about 5cm/2in. Leave spaces between them as access points for small creatures coming to the pond to drink or feed.

Ideally you should also place a geotextile mat over the surface of your liner before you fill it, to protect it from the sun and to help prevent damage from any small stones. Top that with a layer of pond compost, stone-free soil or subsoil mixed with sand – about 15cm/6in thick – on the base to create a planting medium and a habitat for pond life. The soil on the base of any pond must be fairly impoverished, or the nutrients in the soil will feed algae, which will discolour your water and take the oxygen needed for other life.

Now you can fill your pond. If you use tapwater, leave it for a week for the chlorine to evaporate and minerals to disperse before planting. You should not need to add any creatures, it is surprising how quickly water-loving creatures will find a new pond, but you can speed up the process by adding a few handfuls (or bucketfuls depending on the size of the pond) of silt and mud from an established pond. This will contain dozens of pond creatures, from the small to the microscopic.

If you garden on heavy clay, for once you have an advantage because you can make a pond just by digging a hole, firming the clay, and adding water. A clay pond is the best possible base for plant and pondlife, which will colonise it immediately. Even if clay is not your natural soil, you can buy pond liners made of clay granules sandwiched between two membranes (marketed as Bentonite lining), which you use in the same way as plastic lining. It is easy to lay, lasts well and heals itself when

punctured (unlike plastic), but it is quite pricey. Another alternative is to buy Bentonite clay bricks and line your hole with them, closely packed together, but this is rather time-consuming for a large pond. The third method is to buy powdered clay, mix it into a thick paste and spread it like mud over the hole you have dug. But this takes even longer than mixing and laying concrete, is costly and is probably only appropriate for quite a small pond. It does however look entirely natural, and will provide an excellent base for a wildlife pond.

Whether you have natural clay, or you are introducing it, you need to 'puddle' a clay-lined pond well before adding water. This simply means treading it down so that there are no cracks and crevices – it replicates the traditional method of driving cattle into a dew pond to firm it. Clay-lined ponds are ideal for school and community projects, as everyone enjoys racing around stamping the clay flat!

Pondlife

Within days of putting water in a pond you will find pond-skaters and water boatmen appearing, and if you have brought a bit of mud, weed and water from a local established pond you will also get pond snails, water fleas, water spiders, diving beetles and fairy shrimps, all of which do a valuable job keeping your water clear of algae. Once a pond gets established it will attract sedge or caddis flies, and their larvae are also very good cleaners, eating the detritus that falls into a pond before they form cocoons and emerge as slightly dull-looking, pale brown butterflies.

Dragonflies will visit any sunny pond that has a mixture of deep and shallow water

and is well planted with both floating and emergent plants. They either lay their eggs on plants or straight into the water, and spend most of their life as carnivorous larvae, only emerging for reproduction. Damselflies and dragonflies used to be very common, but they have suffered hugely with changing land use, as they relied on traditional wetland habitats, farm ponds and drainage ditches, as well as sunny open water. These are magical creatures, part of the most ancient group of insects on this planet, and are believed to have changed little over the past 300 million years. They are astonishingly accomplished fliers, and it is fantastic to watch them skimming and wheeling, grabbing smaller flying insects with their bristly legs and eating them with their huge jaws.

It probably will not be long before frogs appear in your pond, as shallow garden ponds are their ideal homes. Their numbers have declined drastically in the countryside, owing to changes in land use and agricultural practice and pollution, but overall they are increasing in number, thanks to gardeners. If they do not appear, any pond-owning friend or neighbour will probably be able to provide you with overspill from their own pond, as female frogs lay thousands of eggs, though only a tiny fraction survive weather and predators to become adult frogs. Moving spawn from the wild should only be considered where a pond is about to be destroyed.

The common frog, common and natterjack toads and three species of newt – palmate, smooth and great-crested – together make up Britain's native amphibian population. Their life cycle means they need a dual habitat – a pond where they can lay their eggs and surrounding dry land containing slugs, snails and insects to eat, along with cover to hide from predators and a place to shelter for the winter. The edge of woodland, rough grass or scrubland is perfect, and you will often find amphibians hiding under decaying logs or stones. Toads, newts and most frogs will overwinter in sheltered places on land. Frogspawn is laid in tapioca-like clumps, while toadspawn is laid in long strings.

Newts will usually eventually appear in a pond of their own accord, although toads may take a while to arrive, as they tend to be shy of newly established ponds and prefer the mature planting and cover of an established piece of water. Never try and import great crested newts or their spawn, as they are protected under the Wildlife and Countryside Act 1981 and neither the creatures nor their habitat should be destroyed, damaged or disturbed in any way. Newts lay their eggs wrapped individually on leaves of water plants, so you should not take water plants from the wild either.

Mosquitoes and midges breed by ponds, encouraging bats and other predators to visit on warm evenings. Toads and frogs are the best natural defence against garden slugs and snails, and hedgehogs will hide in the lush foliage beside a pond,

Opposite page: The great crested newt requires damp undergrowth for shelter, as well as water in which to breed.

also preying on slugs. Add to these the birds you will attract, and all the winged and scuttling visitors calling in for a drink, and you soon realise how a pond really does make a difference.

If you have slow-moving water and a clay-lined pond, you may be fortunate enough to attract water voles, which are becoming increasingly rare as the number of suitable waterside habitats has shrunk, and also because of the introduction to the UK of their predator, the North American mink. Water voles are often mistaken for rats but are altogether more desirable, with a blunter nose, plumper face, smaller ears and a shorter tail; they make a characteristic plopping noise when they enter water. Water voles need plenty of grassy cover on pond and stream banks and eat grasses, reeds and sedges; they make their homes in burrows in waterside banks. They prefer clean, slow-moving water, with quiet streams being their habitat of choice, but they may appear in still ponds, given the right vegetation and other sources of water nearby.

Planting a pond

Plant aquatic plants between late April and early September, and never take plants from the wild, instead get them from other pond-owners or reputable suppliers. Use a variety of plants, some with erect stems, some floating plants to provide shade, and submerged plants to oxygenate the water.

Oxygenating plants are the key to a healthy pond, as they compete against algae for nutrients in the water and deprive them of their nourishment. Steer clear of Canadian pondweed *(Elodea canadensis)*, although it is widely sold in garden centres. It is very invasive and you will be constantly battling to remove it. Easily available oxygenating plants include spiked milfoil *(Myriophyllum spicatum)* and curled pondweed *(Potamogeton crispus)*. The buttercup relative, water crowfoot *(Ranunculus aquatilis)*, is a tall plant which roots on the bottom and has submerged leaves. You can plant bottom-rooting plants straight into the soil on the base of the pond, but it is often more convenient to plant in shallow trays filled with rough soil and covered with gravel, which will prevent the soil dispersing.

Next add some floating plants with large leaves, to provide shade on the surface of the water. This shade will prevent algae forming and provide a suitable environment for some pond creatures, such as water snails, which stick their eggs to the undersides of the leaves. Water lilies are prime candidates, as well as amphibious bistort.

There are a whole range of plants suitable for planting around the shallow edge. These include yellow flag irises *(Iris pseudacorus)*, marsh marigolds *(Caltha palustris)*, water forget-me-nots *(Myosotis palustris)*, bog beans *(Menyanthes trifoliata)*, water violets

(Hottonia palustris) and brooklime *(Veronica beccabunga)*. Unless you have a very large pond, or lake, avoid common reed *(Phragmites australis)*, bulrush *(Typha)* and New Zealand water stonecrop *(Crassula helmsii)*, as these can be difficult to control.

Pond maintenance

If you plant a good variety of oxygenating plants, your pond should stay reasonably clear without much attention. However, it is not an instant process and it can take a year or two for a still water pond to clear, particularly if it has been initially filled with tapwater, which encourages algae to proliferate. During the first couple of years the water may turn a variety of colours, from murky grey, to green, to alarming reddish orange during the growing season, although the algae population will decrease as nutrients in the water are used up and their predators increase.

Blanket weed, a surface coating of thick matted algae, is a particularly unsightly nuisance in many young ponds. Eventually pond snails will keep it under control, but initially you will have to clear it, as it locks up the oxygen that pond species need and can even choke out sunlight. It is easy to remove with a stick or rake handle, just wind it round and lift it off. You will probably also need to clear duck weed from nutrient-rich water – rake it off the surface gently – and water fern *(Azolla)* may try to establish itself, but should be picked off regularly. All these problems will lessen as the pond matures. Whenever you remove weed, leave it on the pond edge for at least a day before

putting it on your compost heap. This gives small aquatic creatures the chance to crawl out of it and back into the water.

However murky, weed or algae-ridden your water looks when you are trying to get a pond established, you should not buy proprietary pond-clearing chemicals from garden centres. As with other additives, they offer a quick fix, but have adverse long-term consequences as they alter the balance of the water. They will harm the natural pond life you are trying to establish, and will set you back years in your attempts to create a sustainable pond. If the colour of your water really troubles you, immerse a lump of well bound barley straw in the pond. This will encourage the growth of bacteria that attack the algae in the water. However, the best advice is to leave well alone, apart from rudimentary clearing if necessary, and let nature take its course.

The best time for cleaning, clearing and repairing a pond is always in autumn, when pond activity is fairly slow but before it becomes dormant. And every pond will need some annual maintenance to stop it becoming overcrowded. Ideally plants should take up about a quarter of the pond's area; if they are much denser the organisms in the pond will not be able to function efficiently to clean and clear the pond, and some forms of aquatic life will proliferate at the expense of others. Try to remove loose vegetation every autumn, and every two or three years you will need to lift and divide rhizomatous perennials, such as iris and reeds, and remove excess submerged and floating plants. If your pond is overhung with trees you must give it a good annual clean after leaf fall in autumn, as decaying leaves introduce too many nutrients into the water. Clear away the leaves carefully by hand or with a rake, but try not to remove much silt, as it is home to many species of pond inhabitants, including the larvae of dragonflies and damselflies.

Sometimes old ponds leak and have to be cleared then mended or re-lined. Remove all the pond life and plants carefully and transfer into an old bath or suitable container,

RECOMMENDED WETLAND PLANTS

Acorus calamus (**Sweet flag**)

Angelica sylvestris (**Angelica**)

Calla palustris (**Bog arum**)

Caltha palustris (**Marsh marigold**)

Cardamine pratensis (**Lady's smock**)

Eupatorium cannabinum (**Hemp agrimony**)

Filipendula ulmaria (**Meadowsweet**)

Hypericum elodes (**Marsh St Johns wort**)

Iris pseudacorus (**Yellow flag**)

Lychnis flos-cuculi (**Ragged robin**)

Lysimachia vulgaris (**Yellow loosestrife**)

Lythrum salicaria (**Purple loosestrife**)

Mentha aquatica (**Water mint**)

Menyanthes trifoliata (**Bogbean**)

Myosotis scorpioides (**Water forget-me-not**)

Potentilla palustris (**Marsh cinquefoil**)

Primula elatior (**Oxlip**)

Primula vulgaris (**Primrose**)

Stachys palustris (**Marsh betony**)

Trollius europaeus (**Globe flower**)

Valeriana officinalis (**Common valerian**)

Opposite page: Primulas, ferns and many iris grow best where their roots are not constantly submerged in water.

then repair and refill the pond. If you really cannot repair it, it may be best to fill it with earth and turn it into a wetland habitat.

Wetland gardens

Where it is not practical to have a pond you may be able to construct a wetland or marshy garden, which is also a very valuable habitat for amphibians, insects and the birds they attract, and may be more suitable if you have very young children.

Choose a sunny spot on level ground, away from overhanging trees. Dig a hollow with gently sloping sides to a depth of 30–60cm/1–2ft. The bottom should be as level as possible, and you must remove sharp stones and jutting roots. Make a trench all round the hollow about 15cm/6in deep and 30cm/1ft from the edges. Line the bottom and sides of the basin carefully with plastic liner, estimating how much you need just as for a pond. The length will be twice the depth plus the length of the wetland, and the width will be twice the depth plus the width; leave 45cm/18in overlap to bury in the trench. The quality of the liner is less crucial than for a pond as it does not need to be watertight, just to provide a moist environment, and it will not be degraded by sunlight as it will be permanently covered with soil.

Make a few drainage slits at the deepest part of the hollow, each should be about 25cm/10in long, 30cm/1ft apart. These will allow surplus water in the wetland to drain, as marshland plants will complain if they have to sit in airless stagnant water. Then refill the hollow to about a couple of centimetres below the surrounding soil level with the soil you have excavated, mixed with a bit of garden compost or muck. Unlike a pond, the soil should be nutrient rich and moisture-retentive. However, if you are making a wetland garden in an area of predominantly acid soil, this is a special case and you should add peat moss rather than rich soil, and plant with acid bog-loving plants that fit your local ecology. Never use peat, because of environmental considerations.

Next, water the soil thoroughly. An acid bog should always be watered with rainwater, which is slightly acidic, while tapwater is alkaline, because of the minerals and calcium it contains. The wetland soil does not need to be completely saturated, but leave it to settle for a week before planting anything, and do not let it dry out completely – although most species will survive seasonal changes as the majority of aquatic creatures need wet areas to breed in spring, some need to live in water through the winter but inhabit undergrowth in drier ground at other times. In very hot weather you will need to water gently, and you should mulch over the winter with compost or leaf mould to prevent the ground from freezing solid.

8 Woodland and shrubs

Garden design changes with the times. There is nothing new in this, and while some trends support diversity, others are as harmful to wildlife as modern agricultural practices. There is nothing wildlife-friendly about gardens that contain no more than a few exotic blooms set in a sea of clever paving or neatly mown grass, with brightly painted fences or concrete block walls, however cleverly disguised. The only good reason to have decking is where it provides a sheltered corridor for wildlife to run underneath – but that is often the time when people take it out, thinking it is sheltering vermin. Fortunately the vogue for overly contrived gardens seems to be waning in favour of a slightly more relaxed style, and it is definitely time to reassess the value of trees and shrubs.

Trees can be beautiful and dramatic, elegant and delicate, and gardeners have always valued them for their ability to create height and focus, plus add structure and shade, ornament and fruit. Recently their ecological role in cleaning the atmosphere and helping to stabilise climate change has become widely respected. We need to stop looking at garden trees as isolated specimens, and respect the way they interact with other species to create an ideal environment for wildlife, while maintaining their aesthetic appeal.

Trees have always been appreciated; however, shrubberies have had a very different image. They have been around for at least 150 years, their popularity peaking in the late nineteenth and early twentieth centuries. As gardens got smaller, the appeal of the shrubbery lessened and they are now associated with rather static planting which is less popular than the changing display that clever planting of herbaceous perennials can produce. Fortunately, herbaceous beds can be wonderful for wildlife, particularly as cafés; however, shrubberies have so many advantages that they deserve a second look.

A shrubbery demands far less maintenance than an herbaceous bed, it gives shelter from prevailing winds and can act as a permanent living screen for unsightly corners, it also makes an attractive backdrop to the rest of the garden. A shrubbery provides year-round cover, as well as a rich harvest of blossoms and berries in spring and autumn. In addition, the areas of shade and sunshine and the fact that the ground is rarely disturbed, allows creatures to shelter in comparative privacy. So include some shrubs in your garden or, best of all if you have the space, combine trees and shrubs and create a habitat that resembles the species-rich edge of a woodland.

The woodland edge

Woodland through much of northern Europe has suffered a gradual decline since the pressures of increasing industrialisation in the nineteenth century took people away from the land, leaving woods to become neglected and overgrown. After the First World War they were even more neglected and, instead of traditionally managed native woodland, huge tracts of land were planted with coniferous trees, mainly non-native species cut to provide timber – the only native conifers are juniper and yew.

Dense coniferous woodland is not a productive wildlife habitat. A coniferous plantation is dark and has few plants on the woodland floor, as conifer needles take years to rot and produce very acid compost. Many of our native species of wildlife could not survive naturally, although conifers may have helped the red squirrel and some birds thrive. Fortunately, conifers are nowadays usually planted in smaller blocks interspersed with native broad-leaved trees. When the conifers are felled, the oaks and beeches can be left to form open woodland, similar to the original woodland of Britain.

Another significant type of deciduous woodland is landscaped woodland. This was planted from the sixteenth century onward when great houses were built and woodlands were planned by landscape architects as part of the grand design. Unfortunately, many of these woods are planted with non-native trees and shrubs, which was unhelpful to our native wildlife that had evolved over thousands of years and depended on native plants. If non-native plants take up too much space, squeezing out the native plants which provide a food supply, wildlife is forced to move, and this leads to a decrease in numbers. Some non-native plants, like buddleia *(Buddleja davidii)* and most pyracanthas are good for wildlife, but many more, such as rhododendron are invasive and harmful. It is difficult to find a wood in England that contains no non-native species.

Fortunately, gardeners can help preserve the wildlife that is threatened by habitat loss. Woodland was once the preferred home for thousands of creatures. It is the most versatile habitat in nature, providing food and shelter for every kind of creature, from tiny insects to large mammals. The woodland edge has always been one of the most important wildlife habitats of all. Its mixture of open areas and cover, sunlight and shade, plus the diversity of shrubs, trees and wildflowers, make the ideal environment for a host of small mammals and insects.

When we think of traditional woodland, most of us imagine the sound of birdsong and picture sheets of bluebells, primroses, wild garlic and stands of butchers broom covering the ground, with swarms of butterflies flitting about in the sunlight. It is a nostalgic image, and sadly one which is becoming increasingly rare in reality. Which

Above: Primulas edging this bark path echo natural woodland planting,

makes it even more important to emulate this habitat in order to encourage and preserve the species which make it their home.

Few gardeners have the space to plant a whole wood, but it is possible to create an environment that reflects a woodland edge by planting just one or two carefully chosen trees and a few shrubs. This habitat will prove attractive to a much wider range of creatures than those inhabiting sunnier beds and more open spaces.

The most successful woodland management for wildlife is coppicing. This is a centuries-old system of cutting trees and shrubs down to just above ground level (about 45cm/18in) every few years to encourage them to send up fresh, straight shoots. This technique encourages a wonderfully diverse range of fauna and flora, as it provides for an almost perpetual cycle of growth and renewal. The light that coppicing allows to the ground beneath the trees in spring encourages the ground-covering woodland plants which flower early, then, as the shoots grow, the denser canopy later in the year provides plenty of shade and shelter. As coppicing has become rarer, there have been many wildlife casualties, including nightingales. This is a great loss, as there are few things more thrilling than the clear, sweet sound of a nightingale trilling away.

Above: *Prunus* in blossom underplanted with banks of spring flowers create a woodland feel.

Butterflies and moths also need the sunlight and shade provided by managed woodland – their larvae are nourished by foliage in the shade while the adults feed from flowers in open sites. And so, as old woodlands deteriorate or disappear, a whole host of insects, moths and butterflies, plus many small mammals, such as bats and dormice, struggle to maintain a foothold in a few isolated areas.

Gardeners have not usually thought that such forestry techniques as coppicing have much relevance in a smaller space, and trees have generally been seen as specimens and focal points rather than as interdependent pieces in the bigger garden system. However, we have a lot to learn. Coppicing is a technique ideally suited to small gardens as it keeps the trees at a manageable size and maintains variety during the different stages of growth – providing conditions which create the perfect environment for the growth of other plants, and for butterflies, birds and hosts of small mammals. From the aesthetic viewpoint, coppicing also creates interesting stem shapes and patterns connecting the canopy of leaves above with the planting on the ground, and the stems of young trees can be particularly attractive. Another advantage of coppicing is that you will have a plentiful supply of straight sticks, useful as garden stakes.

Even if you do not choose to plant trees for coppicing, you can mimic the coppiced habitat, with its stratified vegetation and areas of light and shade, by planting to imitate a woodland edge. The aim is to end up with several layers of vegetation, one above the other, and a floor rich with decaying matter. The woodland pattern of gardening is not only excellent for wildlife, it is also very low maintenance, as it requires very little intervention by the gardener once it is established. The interaction between the plants themselves will determine its success.

The major performers are the trees. The shade they cast, their height and density, and the seasonal growth cycles of their leaves and roots control the vegetation that grows and thrives beneath them. When choosing trees it is very important to select a range of natives, such as oak, lime, alder, willow, birch, rowan and hazel, as these will support the widest range of wildlife. Native plants are crucial because they have evolved along with our native wildlife and reciprocal relationships have developed. Insects, in particular, have very specific food requirements, and the grubs of many will only eat the leaves of a particular native species. Although caterpillars and insect larvae may not seem the most fascinating part of your wildlife garden they are vital, as the more insects you have, the more insect-feeding birds, bats and small mammals you will attract. Some birds also rely on the fruit and seeds of natives for food.

The other crucial advantage of native plants is that they have developed to withstand our climate and conditions, so they are usually well adapted to accommodate all that the weather can throw at them without too much complaint – from flood to drought, freezing cold to baking hot. Also, although they provide food for lots of creatures, they are unlikely to be seriously damaged by their role as food provider in the way that more exotic plants can be.

But, as long as you include a fair range of natives it is absolutely fine to include your favourite non-native plants. These will provide some food and shelter and, after all, your garden should be designed to provide you with maximum enjoyment, as well as the creatures that visit it.

Layer upon layer

So where do you start? Your aim is to create a multi-layered area of vegetation with shade and sunlight, and with cover at ground level. A patch of 0.1 hectares/$\frac{1}{4}$ acre or

---

MANAGEABLE NATIVE TREES FOR A GARDEN WOODLAND EDGE HABITAT

Acer campestre (**field maple**) Fast-growing lime-tolerant small tree with rich golden autumn colour. Lime tolerant. Supports many insects and birds. Grows to 8m/25ft.

Alnus glutinosa (**common alder**) Fast-growing slender tree with purple catkins full of pollen in early spring. Popular seed source for many small birds. Thrives in damp soils. Supports more than 80 species of insects. Grows to 15m/50ft.

Betula pendula (**silver birch**) Adaptable hardy tree, noted for its silvery bark and elegant drooping branches. Yellow leaf colouration in autumn. Supports around 150 insect species. Old trees attract woodpeckers for the insects beneath the bark. Prefers well-drained soil. Grows to 20m/70ft.

Betula pubescens (**downy birch**) Hardy tree, slightly darker bark than silver birch, and downy twigs. Prefers damper conditions. Supports about 100 insect species. Grows to 20m/70ft.

Castanea sativa (**sweet chestnut**) Fast-growing tree with large mid-green leaves and yellow catkins in summer. Produces sweet chestnuts. Suitable for coppicing. Grows to 30m/100ft.

more may be able to host a tall layer of large trees with a shorter growing layer beneath, and finally shrubs and ground cover plants, but in most gardens one layer of trees on top of a few shrubs or even woody climbers is enough. In a small garden, be content with small trees, a few nectar- and berry-producing shrubs, and wildflowers at ground level.

First decide on the top layer of tree cover. Apart from space, your soil type and conditions will narrow your choice slightly. For example, beech and oak will thrive in a dry garden, while alders, willows and birch prefer a slightly damper spot; also, beech grows best on limestone, although it will not object to heavier soil once it is established.

Most native trees will manage in most soils; however, you need to take care with feeding and watering to give them a good start if they are growing in less than ideal conditions. This is particularly true where you are planting a garden by a newly built house, as the soil is likely to be fairly impoverished; also gardens in heavily built up areas can have drainage problems and are particularly prone to drying out very quickly.

The more predatory birds, including magpies, crows, rooks and even birds of prey, live in tall trees and more open spaces, while the small birds they prey on will be safe in shrubbier denser cover. Steer clear of the biggest forest trees in a small space, although one or two specimens of a largeish tree such as beech *(Fagus sylvatica)*, hornbeam *(Carpinus betulus)* or white willow *(Salix alba)* can make a small space seem bigger. The disadvantage is that a large tree will also use a lot of nutrients, cast shade and so may deprive a significant proportion of a small garden of light, space and sustenance.

Few plants apart from early spring-flowering bulbs, will thrive beneath the dense and spreading canopy of a mature forest tree. Also, perhaps more pragmatically, if you place a large forest tree too near a house you can cause severe problems in a dry year, when the roots can damage foundations in their search for water. So if you want an oak *(Quercus robur)*, ash *(Fraxinus excelsior)* or lime *(Tilia cordata)* in a smallish garden, you must keep them small by coppicing them every three or four years, and growing them as shrubby trees or incorporating them into mixed hedges.

For most gardens you will probably want to stick with small or medium sized trees, and there are many attractive natives that are easily manageable. Native trees have not been particularly popular in recent decades in any but large gardens, because nurseries offer such a range of exotics which have very seductive qualities. The most common question asked by would-be tree purchasers in garden centres is: "Does it flower?" This explains the popularity of the ubiquitous Japanese cherries, which are a cloud of bright blossom in spring. Although this is a fabulous spectacle, it is worth asking

Opposite page: The male catkins and female flowers of the common alder, beside the aged open fruits.

whether two or three weeks of spectacular blossom on a large plant is enough of a reward in a small garden for a fairly insignificant contribution the rest of the year. This obsession with blossom is curious, most people buy herbaceous plants or sow annuals for their long flowering season, but these are much less obtrusive than a tree when they are not performing.

Trees should be appreciated for dozens of other qualities beyond obvious flowers – the colour of their shoots, their leaves, shape, habit, bark, catkins, berries, seeds and seasonal colour, as well as their associations with wildlife. An obvious choice for a small garden is silver birch *(Betula pendula)*, which grows fast, looks marvellous all year round and casts a light shade, allowing other plants to thrive beneath it. It is also a magnet for insects, and when it matures green woodpeckers seek it out to peck for the grubs lodged in its bark. The prolific seed-bearing English alder *(Alnus glutinosa)* is a fine addition to a damp garden, and is particularly valuable to finches in autumn. Smaller flowering and fruiting natives such as rowan *(Sorbus aucuparia)* and bird cherry *(Prunus padus)* are very good value for birds and insects and cast a frothy, light shade rather than forming a heavy canopy.

Cherry blossom is particularly enjoyed by many butterflies and birds, especially bullfinches, which descend in flocks in spring. An under-rated tree is the wild service tree *(Sorbus torminalis)*, with maple-like leaves, spring blossom and autumn fruit. Field maple *(Acer campestre)* makes an equally fine addition to a woodland edge or top level of a shrubbery, or it can be added to a native hedge. It makes a generous shaped tree with wonderful colour in autumn.

Crab apple *(Malus sylvestris)* is a very useful small tree, covered in pink blossoms in spring and clusters of tiny apples in late summer. It supports dozens of insect species as well as providing fruit for birds and mammals. Although elder *(Sambucus nigra)* is generally considered rather a scruffy unassuming little tree, its scented summer flowers and deep black, juicy fruit attract numerous insects and birds, as well as human foragers. I also treasure it for its place in folklore. It was once known as the countryman's medicine chest, as every part of the tree was used as some remedy or other, and it was also believed to be able to ward away witches and bad spirits. If you have room, do include an elder among your more striking specimens, and if the slightly straggly shape does not appeal, grow a climber such as a dog rose *(Rosa canina)* through it on a sunny edge. Actually any clambering rose would do, even if not a native species, birds, insects and mice will be just as happy with its flowers and hips. You do not need to be too purist about only including natives, just make sure you have a good selection.

MANAGEABLE NATIVE TREES FOR A GARDEN WOODLAND EDGE HABITAT

Corylus avellana (**hazel**)
Lambstail catkins in early spring provide an early source of pollen. Nuts for mice and squirrels in autumn. Supports birds, butterflies and more than 60 insects. Grows to 6m/20ft.

Fraxinus excelsior (**ash**)
Fast-growing tree with dark green leaves and large fruit clusters in autumn. Will form a good windbreak. Supports many birds and insect species. Grows to 30m/100ft.

Ilex aquifolium (**holly**)
Dense evergreen tree. Needs male and female to produce generous red berries in winter. Will grow in the shade of taller trees. Supports holly blue butterfly, many insects and birds. Grows to 12m/40ft.

Malus sylvestris (**crab apple**)
Bears pink blossom and green or yellow fruit. Many associated insects and birds. Grows to 8m/25ft.

Populus alba (**white poplar**)
Fast-growing tree with leaves felty white underneath. Good in exposed and coastal areas. Chalk tolerant. Grows to 20m/70ft.

Opposite page: Holly berries are the final choice for birds in a hard winter.

Spacing is very important to achieving the desired environment of dappled shade and sunlight. For most medium sized trees, it is sufficient to plant them around 3m/10ft apart, but for those that form dense canopies, such as beech and hornbeam, leave 4m/13ft between them, otherwise nothing much will be able to survive beneath them once they mature. Holly, juniper and yew provide lots of food and shelter all year, but form very dense growth, so need to be spaced widely.

Planting trees

Trees should be planted in the dormant season, between October and March, and you must be sure to cultivate the ground well, clearing away any perennial weeds to allow the tree the best possible start. If you are planting a sizeable number of trees, and are not in too much of a hurry, it is best to buy bare-rooted specimens and plant them in a well-composted trench. Water them thoroughly. Alternatively, put the whole bunch into moist soil and keep their roots covered for a week or two until you are ready to plant them out. This is called heeling in.

The main advantages of bare-rooted specimens are that they are extremely cheap and tend to establish very strong root systems quickly, and, once established, the trees really do shoot away. Also, they will not have been pre-shaped. The trouble with many container-grown specimens is that they often have their main shoots tipped to promote bushier lower growth, and if you are creating a woodland habitat you want your top layer of trees to grow as nature intended rather than bushing out too soon. However, it is largely a matter of personal choice, and patience, and if you are only planting one or two trees you will probably prefer to buy fairly established container-grown specimens to get things started.

If you are planning a small woodland, rather than just a woodland edge, and planting bare-rooted trees, you will need to wait a year or two before planting the next layer down – the shrubs or lower growing trees. This is because it is vital to give the top layer the chance to make some growth. Dig a generous hole for each tree, at least twice the depth and diameter of the container, insert a stake to the windward side of each newly planted specimen and plant trees to the line they were grown in the nursery – you will see this from a dark line on the trunk. Firm in well and backfill the hole with a mixture of soil and compost, then water thoroughly, and keep doing so while the tree gets established. Always drench the planting area, as surface watering encourages roots to stay near the damp surface rather than mining deep.

Do not make the mistake of thinking that your job is done once you have planted and watered the trees. A woodland habitat will not take care of itself simply because

Opposite page: Bright red fruits of the spindle tree split to disgorge vivid orange seeds.

MANAGEABLE NATIVE TREES FOR A GARDEN WOODLAND EDGE HABITAT

Sorbus aucuparia (**mountain ash/ rowan**) Medium-sized, hardy tree. Producing clusters of white flowers in early summer. These are followed by large bunches of orange berries in autumn which attracts many birds. Good autumn foliage. Many associated insects. Tolerant to exposed conditions and will reach 15m/50ft.

Sorbus torminalis (**wild service tree**) Medium-sized tree with glossy green, lobed leaves. Looks like a maple but is covered with white flowers in spring and brown fruits in autumn, with glorious yellow-orange and brown leaf colour. Grows to 6m/20ft.

Tilia cordata (**small-leaved lime**) Tree with rounded habit and heart-shaped glossy leaves, dark green above and light green beneath. Cream scented flowers in late summer. Suitable for damp positions. Supports many insect species. Grows to 30m/100ft.

Opposite page: *Viburnum x bodnatense* 'Dawn' is a mass of scented flowers from midwinter before leaves appear.

it is a "natural" part of your garden. You need to keep on top of weeds here just as much as in any other newly planted part of your garden. Even if you decide to leave patches of nettles and willowherb for the creatures that feed off them, you must give your trees – and later shrubs and ground cover plants – the chance to get established without competition. The easiest way to keep the newly planted trees reasonably weed-free is to mulch well around them with compost, leaf mould, bark or wood chippings. Some people in sheep-farming areas use woollen fleeces, as farmers are often happy to supply them for next-to-nothing and they will eventually degrade. Non bio-degradeable alternatives are also possible, such as specially produced tree mats, or porous plastic, or you can use strips of old carpet – though this is not very attractive.

A word of warning. Never plant right against a boundary fence, instead leave a gap of at least 45cm/18in – the roots of any tree will eventually spread as wide as its crown, and you cannot tell what might happen in your neighbour's garden over the years.

Shrubs

Include some natives in your shrubbery layer, which should provide cover and food, and can also be ornamental from spring to winter. The native barberry *(Berberis vulgaris)* is less showy than its many garden relatives, but hardy, accommodating and provides numerous dark berries particularly favoured by blackbirds – as well as dense cover. The native dogwood *(Cornus sanguinea)* is much less widely grown than the dozens of specimen varieties, but it also has attractive foliage that colours well in autumn, and the trademark creamy white flowers and black berries are hugely attractive to many birds and insects.

One of my favourite woodland edge shrubs is the spindle tree *(Euonymus europaeus)*, which should be included in every garden, either as a shrub or part of a hedge. Its wood was traditionally used for spindles, but its magic is the curiously shaped, pinkish-red fruits which droop in small clusters before splitting open to reveal brilliantly orange seeds. Many insects colonise this bush, and birds adore it.

Although potentially invasive, both broom *(Cytisus scoparius)* and gorse *(Ulex europaeus)* love the sunny edge of woodland and provide valuable food for many insects and butterflies, as well as a glorious, glowing yellow colour. The wayfaring tree *(Viburnum lantana)* and guelder rose *(Viburnum opulus)* merit places in any garden woodland edge or hedge, with their profusion of blossoms and berries. Many of the garden cultivars of Viburnum are also extremely attractive to birds and pollen-seeking insects, particularly the sweetly scented, early flowering varieties such as *Viburnum bodnantense* 'Dawn'. I once counted more than forty birds balancing among the

flowers of a large bush outside my sitting room window, a glorious sight in late winter. Buddleias can also be planted on the sunny edge of a shrubby layer. They may not host many insects but they are such a magnet for butterflies that they are irresistible.

Berrying and fruit-bearing plants attract hordes of insects and birds for food and nesting. Most fruiting shrubs and trees will attract members of the thrush family, blackbirds, fieldfares, robins and redwings, and maybe even waxwings and warblers. Birds always go for black and red berries first, moving on to orange, white and pink. So to keep a supply of food over a longer period, it is worth choosing some red-berried species for autumn, and some other colours for later in the season, when food is particularly scarce. Firethorns *(Pyracantha)* are attractive from their summer blossoms to dense summer and autumn berries, and their thick cover provides good nesting opportunities. Another excellent berrying plant is the rare native cotoneaster *(Cotoneaster cambricus)*, it is slightly less showy than its garden relatives, but much better value as an insect plant.

Some winter flowering shrubs are a boon, such as *Mahonia japonica*, with its generous evergreen foliage, scented yellow panicles and decorative black berries. Dense fuchsia bushes are a particular favourite with house sparrows – which were once so common but are now a species that need promoting. Blackbirds adore laurel *(Prunus laurocerasus)* which, although not native and deeply unfashionable, can be very decorative in a mixed shrubbery. Its large, shiny, evergreen leaves are very striking, and its panicles of creamy scented flowers provide masses of pollen in spring.

Small trees such as hawthorn *(Crataegus monogyna)* or hazel *(Corylus avellana)* can be kept to shrubby proportions, providing blossom, nectar, pollen and seeds – wonderful for insects, as well as butterflies and birds. As long as you include a good range of native plants, feel free to plant your own personal evergreen, flowering and fruiting favourites. Remember that butterflies feed in sunlight, so if you want to attract them make sure your chosen nectar-giving shrubs will catch the sun, rather than burying them in shade. Whatever you choose, try to be bold when you plant in late autumn or winter, and chop all shrubs back to within a few inches of their lowest shoots to encourage them to branch out as near to the ground as possible.

On the ground

Give your trees and shrubs two or three years to get established before you try and establish the woodland floor planting of spring bulbs and wildflowers. These need the partial shade of overhead foliage and will not establish themselves without the necessary shading. Meanwhile, attend to the "floor" itself, which should also mimic

---

USEFUL NATIVE SHRUBS FOR A WOODLAND EDGE

Berberis vulgaris (**barberry**)
Bears small spring flowers and bunches of reddish black berries in autumn.

Cornus sanguinea (**dogwood**)
Handsome red stems, clusters of creamy spring flowers and good autumn colour.

Euonymus europaeus (**spindle**)
Small tree or medium-sized open shrub popular with insects and birds. Insignificant flowers are followed by stunning red parcels of berries, that split to drop bright orange fruits.

Rhamnus cathartica (**common buckthorn**)
Large shrub with spiny branches. Small yellow flowers in May are followed by masses of shining black fruits in autumn. Good on chalky soils.

Opposite page: *Mahonia japonica* is valuable for late winter flowers above dense evergreen foliage.

woodland conditions as far as possible, rich with leaf mould, decaying logs and twigs.

This is one area of your garden that really should not be tidied up – have you ever seen anyone sweeping up leaves in a wood? Instead leave leaves and decaying plant material to settle. Some fungus will, in time, establish themselves, and these are natural

recyclers of dead material and magnetic to many small crawling creatures. You will also certainly provide a home for dozens of insects and small creatures. Masses of animal life also make use of dead and decaying wood, burying itself underneath it and tunnelling into it. You may find hedgehogs and other small mammals hiding or hibernating under piles of old logs, and the damp conditions are also popular with young frogs, toads and newts. If you split open a rotting log the soft centre will be packed with beetle larvae and other grubs that have tunnelled inside, and logs may also contain woodwasps, ants, earwigs and woodboring insects, with spiders close at hand to prey on them.

A woodland edge, like a hedge bottom, should in time be a glorious fringe of wildflowers. At ground level there is a huge choice of native plants, most flowering early in the year to make use of the maximum sunlight, before trees and shrubs close their canopies above them. Snowdrops, primroses, bluebells and wood anemones are obvious favourites, and usually quite quick to take hold and spread.

A word of warning, however. Even if you are lucky enough to live in an area where there are still woodlands carpeted with spring wildflowers, you must never ever dig up wild plants. Instead buy them from a reputable supplier, or try and grow them from seed collected from the wild. Be very careful when buying bluebell bulbs and always choose the delicate long stemmed English bluebells *(Hyacinthoides non-scripta)* and avoid the rather heavier bells and broader leaves of Spanish bluebells *(Hyacinthoides hispanica)*. This is because the Spanish bluebells, which have been widely introduced into gardens, have escaped into the wild and are threatening our native species by crossbreeding with them.

Among some of the easiest candidates to establish are stinking hellebores *(Helleborus foetidus)* – which will grow in dry shade – common dog violet *(Viola riviniana)*, lesser celandine *(Ranunculus ficaria)*, and wood forget-me-nots *(Myosotis sylvatica)*.

Woodland flowers are mainly a spring feature before trees and shrubs make competing demands for light and moisture, and summer texture and colour may be easier to provide in other areas of your garden, but the one summer flowering, woodland edge plant you will probably want to encourage is the native purple foxglove *(Digitalis purpurea)*. If foxgloves like you they will spread happily out of the woodland fringe and into your beds, but do not be disappointed if they are a little slow to get going, they are biennial and do not always seed prolifically for a few years. Campions *(Silene* spp.*)*, bugle *(Ajuga reptans)* and wood cranesbill *(Geranium sylvaticum)* are early summer possibilities.

USEFUL NATIVE SHRUBS FOR A WOODLAND EDGE

Rosa canina (**dog rose**)
Thorny rose with fast-growing arching branches. Large white to pink scented flowers in early summer with red glossy fruit in autumn.

Ulex europaeus (**gorse**)
Spiky shrub with dense dark green shoots. Yellow flowers from spring to late autumn. Prefers dry sunny positions and poor soils.

Viburnum opulus (**guelder rose**)
Vigorous shrub with flat clusters of fragrant white flowers forming in early summer and red berries in autumn. Happy in a damp position.

Opposite page: An early black-veined white butterfly feasting at a bluebell flower.

9 Added extras – shelters and feeding stations

Opposite page: Blue tits and great tits are eager visitors to any bird feeder.

Of all the creatures that visit a garden, it is the birds that bring me the most pleasure. They are entertaining and cheerful companions, as well as useful pest controllers. Yet numbers have fallen as many of their natural habitats vanish under tarmac, and deforestation and hedge clearance continue apace. The widespread use of pesticides and herbicides have also taken their toll; however, gardeners can make a huge difference to their welfare with thoughtfully planted gardens, providing good supplies of food and nesting opportunities.

Lay off the pesticides, provide some water, some berried shrubs and trees, a good supply of seedheads and plenty of insects, and birds will flock to your garden. Add some dense shrubs and woody climbers and a tree or two – holly, hawthorn, oak and yew are favourites – and there will be ideal nesting sites to encourage them to stay. But even if you cannot provide all these elements, you can make sure your garden is a good feeding and breeding station by installing a bird table or bird feeders, and placing suitable nest boxes on well-covered walls. It is particularly important to make sure that birds have a source of water in the winter, as they need to bathe regularly to fluff up their feathers as much as possible for insulation. A shallow birdbath is all that is necessary, and it can be as simple as an upturned dustbin lid as long as there is nowhere near where cats can hide, and you keep it full of water and free from ice.

A bird table need be no more than a flat tray with a lip round it, set on top of a sturdy pole or suspended from a branch. It should have hooks around the edge to hang feeders from, and a hole drilled through it to allow water to drain away. The only advantage to tables with roofs is that food will not spoil so easily in bad weather. The best place to put any bird feeding station is where it is clearly visible from the house, so you can enjoy the action. There should be some bushes or trees nearby where birds can shelter and preen. I used to have a table a few metres from my study window, however I found that I spent more hours watching the birds than working so, reluctantly, I moved it to a spot easily visible from the kitchen. This is perfect, as it encourages me to put out food first thing and dawdle over breakfast while watching the birds congregate for their morning feed. Bird feeders can be hung from branches all round the garden and suspended just above windows. In fact when the birds get used to them, you will find they will happily feed very close to humans.

Squirrels can be rather a menace as they will muscle in on any bird food, eating it before the birds have a chance. They are charming to watch as they are such wonderful

aerial acrobats, but they should be dissuaded because, besides eating all the food, they will destroy all but the strongest bird feeders in no time. They are not very tidy feeders either, spilling food on to the ground, which may attract rats. If squirrels do become a nuisance, you will need to feed the birds from squirrel-proof metal feeders, and make it as difficult as possible for them to get on to the bird table. It used to be quite common to see barbed wire twisted around the supports of bird tables to keep squirrels off, however this can harm them, so it is better to place the table away from tall trees, and grease the supporting pole well. If this fails, hang the bird table from a branch that is too light to support the squirrel's weight.

The main threat to small garden birds is attack by cats. So to avoid havoc, make sure your bird table is in an open space with nowhere nearby for cats to hide. Cats are not such agile climbers as squirrels, and an inverted metal cone around the support of a bird table can keep them off, as will the sticky grease used to deter crawling insects from fruit trees. If your garden has masses of cover, hang a bell around your cat's neck, which will at least warn birds of its presence. You can buy electronic cat deterrents, which may work well, but this seems rather a drastic solution even to me – and I confess that I am not a cat lover, precisely because of the damage they cause to birds.

When and what to feed

Feeding garden birds is not pampering them, it is genuinely important to their survival through winter, when food supplies are scarce in all but the most bountiful garden and the cold weather means they need to eat more to stay alive. Tiny birds, such as wrens and bluetits, need to eat almost the equivalent of their own body weight of food every day during a cold spell, just to survive the night and forage. All their waking time during the autumn months is spent searching for food, and their lives depend on finding it. Put out food regularly, twice daily if possible, in the early morning and again in the afternoon. Once you have started feeding you must continue, as birds will begin to rely on your source of food once they have discovered it.

Arguments rage about the rights and wrongs of birds becoming dependent on humans for their food, but we have made them dependent by removing their natural habitats and food sources. Besides which, some species have foraged with humans for centuries – think of how gulls and rooks follow the farmer's plough to see what fare it exposes, and how joyful it is to garden with a robin as a companion as he waits for you to expose earthworms and grubs as you dig and clear.

There is not the same need to provide food from the end of April to early October, as supplies should be plentiful in most gardens; however, recent evidence suggests that it is useful to continue feeding, as you will be supporting adult birds as they work hard to find natural foods to feed their young. By supplementing their diet, the likelihood of adults and their brood surviving and thriving is increased. Greenfinches particularly benefit, as they have a late breeding season, so it helps if food is available in May.

Fill bird feeders with seed mixes and nuts. However, never put out salted peanuts, and only buy your feed from reputable suppliers. Make sure the seed mixes contain plenty of flaked maize, broken peanuts and sunflower seeds with, perhaps, oatmeal. Peanuts are rich in fat and very popular with tits, green finches and house sparrows. If you are lucky, you may also see nuthatches, spotted woodpeckers and siskins on the feeders. Crushed or grated nuts attract robins, dunnocks and even wrens. Small seeds, such as millet, appeal to house sparrows, dunnocks, finches, reed buntings and collared doves; tits, greenfinches and goldfinches choose nuts and sunflower seeds, blackbirds and dunnocks enjoy flaked maize. Oatmeal is good for many birds, but avoid mixes with wheat and barley in them as these will attract large birds, particularly pigeons, and corn should, in any case, only be fed on the ground.

Suet is very popular with tits. So if you have fruit trees, hang suet balls from the branches and you will find that once they have eaten the fat, the tits will move on to the grubs overwintering in cracks in the bark. Tits and some other birds also love coconut halves, which can be hung from bird tables or branches. Once the coconut has been stripped you can fill the shell with bird cake, made by pouring liquid suet or lard over a seed mix and leaving it to go solid in the shell. You can also hang up yoghurt pots filled with this birdcake mixture, or press it between the gaps in pinecones and hang these from your bird table.

You can put out all sorts of kitchen scraps, but nothing salty. Bread is not the best fare for birds, although they consume tons of it each year. It does not matter if it is a bit mouldy, however you should moisten it if it is very dry. Grated cheese is popular with robins and thrushes, and many birds like bacon rinds, but don't put out those from very salted bacon. Bones with some fat or meat attached are good, but magpies will take over the table, and it is best to hang them separately from a tree. Cooked

Below: Greenfinches are particularly susceptible to disease. Clean your birdtable regularly to be safe.

potatoes are valuable, and cooked rice is good, while dry porridge oats or oatmeal are valuable bird food.

Dried fruits, such as raisins and sultanas, or scraps of fruit cake or fruit puddings, are particularly enjoyed by blackbirds, song thrushes and robins, while sliced apples are very popular with thrushes, blackbirds and starlings. A robin's favourite feast is mealworms, which can be bought from bird food suppliers, and these may also attract insect-eating birds, such as pied wagtails.

Never feed dried rice, dried legumes or desiccated coconut. These can kill birds. Cooked porridge oats are also not advisable and although some fruits are popular, avoid citrus fruits and banana skins, and never leave out spicy foods for birds.

Hygiene is important on a bird table. You should clear away any food left on the table in the evening to stop any rodents from feeding and to prevent a mass of stale food from building up. In theory it is a good idea to move a bird table occasionally, as it will attract a mass of birds, some of which will be less healthy than others, so you may be at risk of spreading disease. However, in reality this is not always practical, and as long as you scrub it regularly there really should not be a problem. The area beneath the table may get a bit muddy underfoot by the end of winter as a result of spilt food and birds' feet, but that is a very minor inconvenience.

Manmade breeding sites for birds

Even the most wildlife-friendly gardens can provide extra support with deliberately placed shelters. If you feed the birds, you will also want them to stay in the garden to breed, and you can encourage this by placing suitable nest boxes at strategic points. More than sixty different species have been known to use nest boxes, including bluetits and great tits, nuthatches, house and tree sparrows, spotted flycatchers, robins, house martins, kestrels and even tawny owls. Much depends on where the box is sited and on your surroundings.

Boxes should be fixed to a wall or tree, well out of the reach of cats. Unless there are trees or buildings giving permanent shelter, you should always place them facing between north and east to avoid strong sunlight and the wettest winds. They should also be tilted slightly forwards so any rain will run off easily. House sparrows and starlings will use boxes high up under the eaves of houses, while open-fronted boxes for robins and wrens need to be low down, well hidden by vegetation.

There are all sorts of boxes available, from woven coir to concrete, but in most situations wooden boxes are best. They fit into any surroundings, so are likely to appeal to most birds, they are cheap to buy or easy to construct from any non preservative-treated wood. They are also easy to clean and repair. Most birds choose either boxes with small entrance holes, or open-fronted boxes with a cross piece about 8cm/3in tall from the base at the front and a projection over the roof to keep the rain off.

Small open-fronted nest boxes may attract robins and wrens, and perhaps pied wagtails and spotted flycatchers. However, many garden and woodland birds nest in holes and will be attracted to a nest box with a small hole in the front. What species you attract will depend on its local distribution and population, and on the size of the entrance hole. An entrance hole 28mm/1in in diameter will admit bluetits, great tits, coal tits, tree sparrows and pied flycatchers, while a slightly larger hole (32mm/1$\frac{1}{4}$in in diameter) will attract house sparrows, nuthatches and lesser spotted woodpeckers. Jackdaws and starlings will happily take up residence in a box high on a house wall with a large hole around 10cm/4in diameter, but green and great spotted woodpeckers prefer an entrance about 50 or 60mm/2 or 2$\frac{1}{4}$in. All woodpecker boxes should be mounted as high as possible up a tree.

You will find that most birds adapt the size of the hole once they adopt the box. Some will stop it with mud to make it smaller, more will chip away at it to make it larger – even if it is already a perfectly adequate size to allow them free access. Woodpeckers are the worst culprits, and if you have woodpeckers you will probably need to repair or replace boxes quite regularly. When they find a hollow box, whatever size the entrance hole, they nearly always tap at it. As it sounds hollow they may be searching for the grubs that hide in hollow logs rather than trying to enlarge the entrance hole.

Large nest boxes can accommodate tawny owls and even kestrels, and these are particularly valuable in urban areas, where these birds are becoming increasingly common yet where they may not have suitable nesting sites. A kestrel will nest in a large open-fronted box set high on a wall with a lipped shelf about 150mm/6in square and sides at least the same size, with a slightly overhanging roof. Tawny owls need a large rectangular box with a base of around 200mm/8in square and walls about 750mm/30in high. It should have one end left open, and be mounted under the eaves at an angle of about 45 degrees from the wall.

You do not need to be much of a carpenter to make a bird box, all you are aiming for is a safe weatherproof box, the state of the joints really is not important. But you must hinge the roof of boxes with holes in the front, so you can clean them out easily after the fledglings have left. Either use a non-ferrous hinge or a strip of rubber. You should also drill small drainage holes in the floor of all boxes.

Housemartins make hemispherical nests of mud, so they need a good supply in

Opposite page: Great spotted woodpeckers can become regular visitors to bird feeders, keep them filled daily in winter.

spring. This could come from the margins of a garden pond or you could keep a patch of earth very well watered for them. You can also purchase housemartin boxes to hang under your eaves. These may not be colonised immediately, but once the birds start to use the box, they will probably return year after year, as they are among the many birds that like to return to the same breeding site. If your boxes are occupied by the same species every year you can be sure it is members of the same family returning to breed, but if more than a year goes by without martins, or even tits, returning, it is likely that any new residents will be from a completely different family.

Bat roosts

There are sixteen species of bats in the UK, but of these six are endangered and six are vulnerable, so they desperately need all the help we can give them. Unlike birds, bats do not nest, instead they creep into nooks and crannies; however, they still need somewhere safe, quiet, draught-free, dry and warm to roost and breed. The felling of dead, old and hollow trees has reduced the availability of their natural roost sites, and although bats will always prefer natural tree holes or quiet roof spaces, bat boxes can help. Pipistrelle and brown long-eared bats are the commonest bat species to use bat boxes, although horseshoe bats may be tempted if you are very fortunate, and you may also attract the less common noctule, Leisler's, Natterer's and Daubenton's bats. Bats breed in summer, but they also need warm places where they will be undisturbed through winter hibernation.

To attract bats you need to have a source of water, either in your garden or nearby, and well-stocked flower borders will be appreciated, as they attract the moths bats like to feed on. Insect-rich native hedgerows and woodland edges provide ideal feeding grounds for bats, and flower-rich grass meadows are also perfect for foraging.

You can purchase wooden or cement and sawdust bat boxes, but it is simple to make your own from rough sawn untreated timber. They should last for around ten years, unless they are damaged by squirrels. If squirrels are a problem, use cement and sawdust boxes.

Bat breeding boxes can be made in a similar fashion to a small hole bird nesting box. The difference is that instead of making a hole in the front, you need to leave a gap of at least 15–20mm/$^1/_2$–$^3/_4$in underneath the base of the box for the bats to use as an entrance. A box between 15–20cm/6–8in tall with a sloping roof will suit all species – brown long-eared and noctule bats require the larger size – and it is best if all surfaces are made from rough sawn wood, so that the bats can land and investigate by crawling over the box.

Opposite page: Erect nesting boxes where there is plenty of surrounding cover.

Right: Housemartins like a pond or boggy bed nearby to gather mud for their nests.

Opposite page: A bat box needs to be high off the ground, preferably on the edge of deciduous woodland.

Boxes can be sited in any area where bats are known to feed, but a tree on a sheltered woodland edge or near an old hedgerow is ideal, particularly if there is water close by. Attach them to trees or buildings, in as sheltered a position as possible, and they must get sun for a good part of the day – you will not attract bats with boxes facing north or north east. The higher the box is positioned the better, and most bats will roost at between 3–5m/10–16ft, although brown long-eared bats prefer a box only 1.5m/5ft above the ground. These are very vulnerable to cats – and curious humans – so make sure low-level boxes are placed where they will not be disturbed.

Bats hibernate in winter, when there are few insects for them to feed on, and winter boxes need to provide good insulation. You can make these from hollowed out logs, thick planking or layers of wood sandwiched together with insulating material. They are best situated under the eaves of your house on a sunny wall, or high in a sheltered tree.

It may take a few years for bats to occupy your boxes, and they will never come if there are sites or established colonies nearby, or if the boxes are not sheltered enough. The best way to check for occupancy is to watch the boxes regularly at dusk. If you need to inspect the insides open them very carefully, as bats may be hanging on the top, and before you close the box remove the bats and put them at the entrance where

they can crawl back in. This will ensure you do not trap their feet in the lid. You must not open any boxes between June and mid-August, when bats are giving birth and lactating. In the UK bats are protected under the Wildlife and Countryside Act 1981, and you need a special licence to disturb roosting bats and to handle them, so once bats are known to be roosting in your boxes you should apply for the licence.

Helping other mammals

A country garden will probably provide ample places for a hedgehog to nest – in the cover of a hedge bottom, a pile of leaves or a compost heap – but extra help is always valuable and is particularly important in small town gardens. Hedgehogs are quite happy in town, as long as they have insects and invertebrates to eat, as well as water and somewhere to shelter and nest.

A pile of leaves in a reasonably dry and sheltered spot is ideal, and hedgehogs are also happy hibernating under a wood pile, or in the centre of a compost heap. Hedgehogs will also hibernate in any dark, dry box in a peaceful place. A wooden box camouflaged with leaves or even old carpet can work quite satisfactorily, but it must be left undisturbed, so tuck it away in as secluded a place as possible. Also remember that your garden must provide food, drink and shelter for the hedgehogs to entice them in in the first place. If you want to supplement the hedgehog's diet, particularly valuable in autumn when they are slowing down and preparing for hibernation, do not give them bread and milk but meat scraps – canned dog food is fine and they also seem to like the robins' favourite treats, mealworms. If you do not have a pond in your garden, make sure a bowl of water is always kept full for hedgehogs to drink from. Always check for hibernating or nesting hedgehogs before you clear old woodpiles, light bonfires or turn over compost heaps.

If you have a large garden in the country, you can attract foxes and badgers, rabbits and deer by feeding them in a part of the garden that they cannot damage. You will need to fence in the ornamental and productive parts of your garden as deer will eat the tips off many plants, including young trees, and badgers can do a lot of damage by digging up areas of your grass and flowerbeds to get at invertebrates to eat. Rabbits, of course, will eat any vegetation. Put peanuts and seeds on the ground for deer and badgers, while foxes and badgers will be attracted by meat. One of the delights in observing wildlife is the way different creatures interact with each other. Within a species there will be a rigid pecking order, so you will not, for example, get two male deer or foxes feeding together; however, if you are lucky you may see deer, foxes, badgers and rabbits all feeding happily side by side.

Opposite page: Survival of the fox depends on the availability of food in its territory.

Index

Acknowledgements

Frank Lane Picture Agency
Leo Batten 101
B. Borrell Caslas 31
Michael Clark 179
W. Minderts/Foto Natura 50, 145
R Tidman 107
John Tinning 141, 182
John Watkins 98
R Wilmshurst 120
R. Wilmshurst 32
Roger Wilmshurst 11, 48
Garden Picture Library
Linda Burgess 13
Eric Crichton 81
Juliet Greene 65
Michael Howes 56
Jaqui Hurst 115
Mel Watson 92
Garden & Wildlife Matters 99
John Feltwell 68
John Glover
Design: HRH Leyhill Prison 35
Design: Rupert Golby, Country Living Kitchen
Garden, Chelsea 95 88
Jerry Harpur 91, 109, 114, 116, 123, 164
Design: R. David Adams, Seattle 153
Barnsley House, Gloucestershire 60
Charles Beresford-Clark, Sussex 110
Design: Beth Chatto, Essex 154, 160
Design: Chris Grey-Wilson 8
Design: Susan Houseman 75
Design: Iris Kaplow, Kate Kind's Garden 87
Design: Lady Arabella Lennox-Boyd 27, 82
Design: Mirabel Osler, Shropshire 138
Park Farm, Essex 41
Design: Michael Runge 12
Design: Ernie Taylor, Gt Barr 76
Winfield House 151

Marcus Harpur 29, 62, 72
Design: Jonathan Baillie 94
Feeringbury Manor, Essex 19
Park Farm, Essex 22
Pound Farm House, Essex 44
Andrew Lawson 17, 25, 28, 54, 58, 63, 73, 96, 102, 106, 137, 163
Ashton Wold, Peterborough 113, 122
Design: Miriam Rothschild 129
Rodmarton Manor, Glos 108
Sticky Wicket, Dorchester 119
Design: Sara Woolley 24
Maayke de Ridder
Design: Elspeth Thompson 78, 85
N.H.P.A.
Mark Bowler 142
G J Cambridge 130
Laurie Campbell 127
Bill Coster 170
Stephen Dalton 15, 36, 49, 52, 69, 71, 124
E A Janes 67
E A Janes 126, 134, 158
Mike Lane 169
Alberto Nardi 146
Eckart Pott 147
Mirko Stelzner 4-5
Alan Williams 175
Clay Perry
Design: Kate Cambell, Eye Abbey, Suffolk 16
Photos Horticultural 176
Jason Smalley/www.jasonsmalley.com 46, 132, 149
Woodfall Wild Images
Steve Austin 157
Inigo Everson 178
Bob Glover 14
Nigel Hicks 125
Mike Lane 172, 180
Richard Revels 166